Sin Boldly!

Dr. Dave's Irreverent Guide to Acing the College Paper

by
David R. Williams, Ph.D.

Book design and layout by Andi Harris
Cover illustration by Stilson Greene
Drawing on page 13 by Jamie Rasmussen

Dr. Dave Publishing
P.O. Box 12
Lincoln, VA 22078

ISBN 0-9644419-0-X

APPRECIATION

This book originated out of my desire to avoid wasting too much time teaching grammar and writing in my literature classes at George Mason University. Eager to spend more time with Jonathan Edwards and Ken Kesey and less with punctuation, I began to place short jeremiads on reserve in the library. When I discovered that students were xeroxing these papers at a dime a page, I decided to print my own copies of the entire collection and sell them in the campus bookstore to make a buck. That booklet (now a collector's item) became a word-of-mouth success, used even in composition courses, and I was persuaded to expand the text and to try for a larger market.

I therefore owe my students at George Mason the most. Their horrendous mistakes were my inspiration. Several friends and colleagues also helped to get me organized and to keep me working. Suzanne Melancon was the first professional writer to take my project seriously. Kathy Mitchell was the second. Roger Lathbury also contributed significant advice, as did my son, Nathan. The moral encouragement provided by a host of others can best be exemplified by the words of Dr. Bruce Levy who wrote me saying, "Let's face it: writing courses suck. They know it; we know it. The only way to win them over is to admit to the truth right off the bat."

I may be bats, but here's the truth, at least as I see it.

CONTENTS

INTRODUCTION

Tired of correcting the same mistakes — even in senior papers — year after year, hoarse and in danger of developing throat cancer from endless repetition of the same rules, tired even of my own lame jokes and pathetic attempts to humorize grammar and the writing process, at long last frustrated by the inability of far too many obtuse students to grasp the words of wisdom I have shouted at them through the apparently impenetrable air, I am here casting off all pretense and committing to paper the real rules and regulations that have guided me for years as I grade student papers. Note that many of these rules apply equally well to the grading of exams. In any case, they should certainly help you in your quest for the dearly desired grade you think you deserve.

Many of you, with some justification, are convinced that the rules of composition and grammar are a crock, that they are petty and irrelevant beyond belief, and that the only reason English professors insist upon them is to exercise one brief and feeble moment of power in their otherwise power-less, meaningless, and uneventful lives. There is some truth to that. There is even a school of thought within the English-teaching profession that views grammar as a tool of imperialism, a way for white male culture to impose its values upon others and make them conform to a value system that keeps white males in command. There may be something to that too. And of course there are those who simply ignore such rules, knowing for sure that they will waltz into the executive suite of daddy's firm or will so quickly rise from salesman to CEO that they will always have some secretary to correct their mistakes for them.

Assuming all this is at least in some part true, doesn't that make it all the more important for you to wield the tools of power rather than be at the mercy of someone else's knowledge? There will always be power and there will always be symbols of it. Knowledge of correct grammar and the ability to write are symbols of this power. I can think of no better symbol of power than literacy. Would you prefer the sword? The aristocratic title? Ugly gold medallions on gold chains? A Lincoln Continental? An AK-47? Since we live in a competitive society in which the struggle for survival is primary, power exists, and power will have its symbols. Literacy is a far better tool and symbol of empowerment than any other, even money.

Historically, the teaching of grammar arose as a deliberate effort to provide arbitrary rules to which all people who aspired to middle class gentility could conform. It was thus a means of taking one of the weapons of power away from an hereditary feudal elite and making it available to all the people. It was part of the eighteenth-century revolt against aristocratic privilege, against a world in which a member of the gentry simply by being a member of the gentry set the norm for what was right and proper simply by whatever he did. However much you may hate grammar, think how much better a system ours is in which even the lowest peasant can achieve literary equality by learning rules of writing, spelling, grammar, and diction that are available equally to all. Andrew Jackson, in the years when Noah Webster was trying to stamp equality upon us, resisted this trend proclaiming that he had no respect for the intelligence of a man who couldn't think of more than one way to spell a word. There was a glorious freedom in those days. But equalité has assumed a higher value than liberté. We must all become the same. The ability to write forcefully, convincingly, grammatically is less a tool of privilege than one of the strongest weapons against it. It is the tool that you must have if you are to compete successfully against the spawn of Yale and Harvard.

For those business majors and majorettes out there still not persuaded, let me reveal a secret of one of America's leading business tycoons, a secret that should freeze your souls. In *Minding the Store*, his rags-to-riches story of how he made it to the top of his daddy's business with the help of his daddy's millions, Stanley Marcus, former Emperor of the Nieman-Marcus merchandising empire, lets slip the revelation that he has what he calls "a personal antipathy." What is this shameful prejudice? Dislike of blacks? Fear of Arabs? Hatred for anything in green polka dots? No, his personal antipathy is for the misuse of the personal pronoun after a preposition. He once broke off an engagement to a beautiful and hopeful young lady who almost landed her millionaire until she said in a moment of unguarded passion that there was such great love "between you and I." Off with her head! And then there was the up and coming young junior executive who responded to a generous Christmas gift by thanking Marcus for the lovely vase he had sent "to Helen and I." According to Marcus, he never rose any further in the organization and did not last long, and he never even knew why.

If you do not know what wrong these two sinners had done to justify their being cast out of the garden into the darkness where there is wailing and the gnashing of teeth, then you need the lessons in this little book. Perhaps you are right that the rules of grammar are stupid and arbitrary and that the people who wield them are arrogant and arbitrary. But many of those same arrogant and arbitrary people are out there wielding power. Someday, one of them may be your boss. One of them may be grading your papers this semester. In the interest of survival, if nothing else, you need to be prepared to meet the challenges of this power. As Jimmy Carter once said, "Life is not fair." Victory goes to those who are prepared to deal with life on its own terms, not in terms of some imagined fairness.

Let us get on with it.

CHAPTER 1

Some Really Crude Basics

What Is A College Paper?

Let's admit from the start that by "college paper" we mean a paper for a course in the humanities. The sciences, bless them, have their own peculiar ways of using language which many of us in the humanities find bizarre. Of course, the way some humanists write papers is also beyond belief. One has only to pick up any work by one of the adherents of the modern "deconstructionist" school of literary analysis to see how bad academic writing can get. Forget all that academic jargon. Any college paper you write reflects your opinion and should be in whatever style or voice is most comfortable for you. And whether the paper is for the English Department, History Department, Psychology Department, Religious Studies, or any of the many subsets of the social sciences, the rules here outlined generally apply. Even such pseudosciences as economics and business require papers that are written in English and follow the same general rules and procedures as an essay on Emerson.

That said, it is undoubtedly true that you can get away with more colorful and creative — if not downright peculiar — experiments in a paper for a literature class than in one for an economics class. But even this is not guaranteed. Some English professors imagine themselves as super-sophisticated, scientifically based apostles of some weird school of literary analysis and therefore insist on rigidly exact performances, while some economists are as loose as the proverbial goose. And some of the best scientists write not in science-ese but in clear human speech. Reading Freudians is an exercise in despair and confusion; reading Sigmund Freud himself is a delight. There is a reason for this.

The historian Barbara Tuchman has said that the ability to write well implies the ability to think well. Great minds think and write clearly; secondary minds get confused; inferior minds tie themselves in knots pretending they understand what they clearly can't even grasp. People who understand what they are talking about write in clear simple language intended to communicate ideas from one mind to another. People who do not have a clear idea of what they are talking about try to hide their confusion behind an ink cloud of obscure verbiage. And some superior snots actually write not to communicate but to impress people with how smart they think they are.

Do not, therefore, be afraid to say what you think in plain, simple English. To the truly literate, the use of excessively pompous and complex language indicates cowardice and ignorance, not intelligence. If you cannot understand your textbook, do not despair; the fault may well be the writer's, not yours. In contrast to European intellectuals with their aristocratic heritage, the best American writers from the very beginning gloried in what we call "the plain style." Our greatest American books are not clouds of baroque rhetoric but simple American speech. Think of the dialect in *Huckleberry Finn*, the direct sentences of Ernest Hemingway, the penetrating boldness of James Baldwin, and be not afraid.

The college paper is assigned to determine how well the student has mastered the material of the course, how well the student has understood the significance for good or ill of that material, and how well the student can write about it. Whether for History, English, or whatever, the requirements of good arguments, good evidence, good communication are essentially the same. It is on these requirements that this booklet is focused.

The Format And The Length

Leave all your plastic binders in Miss Hodgebottom's fourth grade classroom. They fall apart scattering pages to the breeze or leaving them to be scrunched up in the bottom of my book bag. They feel like slimy death; they are an expensive environmental disaster. Simply staple an 8.5 x 11 white title page to the front of your paper.

This title page should have a title in the center about a third of the way down. The title should not be in quotation marks unless it is a quotation. It should not be underlined unless it is also the title of a published work. It should say something. "Paper #2" is not a title. In the lower right-hand corner of this title page should be your name, the date, and the name and number of the class.

Do not repeat the title on the first page. The actual first page of text should begin at the top just as any other page does. Nor should you begin the first page halfway down the paper as if there had to be room for a title that isn't there. We professors know padding when we see it. And for the love of Gaia, do not include blank pieces of paper at either the beginning or the end. Play your tricks of illusion with words. I am constantly amused at the students who try to hide their papers in the middle of the pile when they are turning them in, as if we teachers never actually read the things. We do. You can't hide from us. And when we get to yours we will realize with surprising speed that the thick paper handed in was padded by empty sheets on either side. Once so alerted, we will then be on the lookout for padded paragraphs too.

The paper must be typed or whatever the verb is for word-processing. No, we do not allow neat handwriting. There is an absolute universal requirement that you double space. We can recognize triple and even two-and-a-half-line spacing, so don't get cute. Double spacing gives us room to write our penetrating critiques of your mistakes in between the lines. We need all the room we can get.

Standard margins are an inch and a quarter on the sides, an inch and a half top and bottom. Each page should be numbered. I prefer the numbers at the top right, out of the way, to leave room for my own pithy comments.

The length of the paper, of course, should be part of the assignment. If you are not sure, do not be afraid to ask. If you don't know, then chances are very good that others don't know. The rest of the class and the teacher will thank you for clearing up the confusion. An assigned length of two to three pages does not mean one page and a line at the top of the second. It means at least two full pages with the possibility of spillover onto a third. Note that while we hate to discourage eager students, few of us are thrilled to see papers that are several pages longer than the assignment calls for. Learning to be concise is a major part of learning to write. We are glad you have something to say, but keep it under control please. With perhaps 40 4-page papers to grade before tomorrow, we are faced with at least 160 pages to read and edit before dawn. Being able to put yourself in the other guy or gal's sneakers is a universal requirement for success in any endeavor.

I often do not give page lengths, thereby creating great anxiety. This causes problems for me as well. But by giving 8-page assignments to students with four pages worth of knowledge, we English professors actually work against our own instructions. We say, "be brief," "be concise," "don't waste words," and we make fun of bureaucrats who write 30-page memos on how to buy a doughnut. Then we give out assignments that force many students to have to learn how to turn four pages of information into eight pages of words. By doing this, we are in fact inadvertently teaching the very excess of verbiage that we claim to abhor. Instead, I say, define your topic, establish your argument, present the evidence for this argument, rebut any objections, and bring it all to a resounding conclusion. To do all this should take at least four or eight or twenty or whatever is the number of pages I have assigned. If you can do it in fewer than the minimum required, may Allah be merciful. If you require a bit more, I'll try to understand. Do the best job you can.

How Much Work?

Do not even contemplate trying to write the paper in one draft unless it is already 2:00 a.m. and you are so far gone that you don't care what kind of a grade you get as long as the assignment is accepted. The first draft is always just a rough sketch of possibilities.

The very act of writing can itself be liberating. The rough first draft may well be nothing more than a page or two of hastily scribbled impressions. If you have any interest or curiosity at all, whether negative or positive, about a specific character or phrase or event, begin describing it. You will be amazed how soon ideas begin to flow. But under no circumstances should you think of this first effort as any more than the jotting down of rough preliminary notes.

If the first draft then is barely comprehensible, the second draft is your best working paper. This is written once you have a pretty good idea of what you want to do. It is the skeleton of what will become your paper. It is also the hardest one to write. Do not worry here about perfection, for this is also the draft that you will then have to go over carefully to make corrections in logic and organization, to note where better evidence is called for, or what has been left out, or where the argument has wandered off the path. The third draft then comes close to being your finished paper, but this is the copy that needs to be examined closely for typos, grammatical mistakes, misspellings, and other last minute problems.

Ideally, then, your fourth draft should be your final copy. Ok, laugh, but at least you've been told.

Timing Counts!

In graduate school one semester, taking a seminar on William Faulkner from the great Hyatt Waggoner, I had the opportunity to shock a young classmate. She and I and a fellow student were walking along the brick sidewalk outside of class talking about the term papers we had been assigned. Suddenly, she turned and stopped us both in our tracks demanding, "Wait a minute! Are you guys actually saying that you intend to get these papers in on the assigned date?" He and I gave each other puzzled looks and shrugged. She stomped off in a fury saying, "I never heard of such a thing. Why, I've never handed in a paper on time in my life. What are you guys trying to pull?" She didn't return the following semester. He and I are now up to our keisters in sophomore papers.

Deadlines are meant to be taken seriously, not absolutely, but seriously. You are going to have to sit down at some point and do the work, so you might as well determine to do it at the first opportunity instead of the last. There'll be plenty of time for procrastination in the grave. I wish I had the gall of Harvard's Alan Heimert. He once assigned us a term paper that had to be in on April 18. After giving us that date, he drummed his fingers on the table, looked up at the chandeliers, then sighed, "Ok, if you develop pneumonia and your dog goes into labor, I suppose I have to let you have an extra week. There, you've got until the 25th." Then he gritted his teeth, drummed some more, and said, "Alright, alright, if your grandmother dies and the funeral is in Texas, or the government is overthrown and you have to go to Washington to save the republic, I guess I'll have to give you one more week. There! Do not ask for any more extensions. I've given you an absolute deadline and two extensions. If you can't get it in by May first, forget it!"

Still, there will be students who will insist on making excuses and requesting extensions. One of the problems with this is that we teachers have heard them all. I always tell my sophomores at the beginning of my survey course to kiss their grandparents goodby before the final, since so many of them seem to kick off that week. Even if there is a death in the family, you need to grit your teeth and get on with life. How long can a funeral take, anyhow?

We teachers get to be a pretty hard-hearted, cynical bunch. Once a sexy young female from Iran in a writing class came up to me before the mid-term, stood altogether too close, and allowed how she would do "anyzing" for an A. When I suggested that she work harder, she burst into tears and confessed that she had a problem. She was in the U.S, she said, on a grant which required her to get straight As. If she lost the grant, she would have to drop out of school. If she had to drop out of school, she would lose her student visa and have to return to Iran. Since her father had supported the Shah, if she returned to Iran, she would surely be shot. "Well, guess you really had better work harder," I said. She left in a snit. A week later she was back with another story. This time, she said, she would tell me the truth. She had been exaggerating before, but the truth was that her husband was paying her tuition. He did not believe that women should go to college, but if she wanted to go on his money, she had to make straight As or he would beat her. I believed her that time for some reason, but my answer was the same: work harder.

CHAPTER 2

Choosing a Topic

K.I.S.S.

Ray Kroc, the founder of McDonald's, had in his office a sign which read "K.I.S.S." which, he was glad to tell anyone, meant "Keep it Simple, Stupid." Simple does not have to mean simple-minded. Keeping it simple means avoiding the complexity of too many competing, confusing factors. This applies to choosing a paper topic as well as writing a sentence or running a business.

Pick one topic, one argument, that is finite, limited, and can be defined. Do not try to explain everything; it can't be done. Even if you think you know everything, avoid the temptation to put it all in every paper. We college professors do not simply skim the page looking for "points" to put checks next to which we then add up to determine the grade. Narrow in on a specific question, or problem, or character. Pick a word, or a phrase, or an image, or an event. Ask a specific question: "Why does the author use this particular word or image in this paragraph?" "Why did the Americans in Texas declare their independence in 1836 instead of 1835?" "Why does Jesse Jackson prefer the term African-American to Afro-American or black?"

Your analysis of that specific question can then widen to include the larger problems of the text, or of life. Begin with the specific and then expand to the larger contexts, first of the work under consideration, then of the author and his or her world, and then, if you are feeling ambitious, of the cosmic whole. But do not leave us floating in outer space. Keep the original rock from which you started in sight and be sure to return to it by the end.

When you do not have to answer the question of what the entire text is all about, the problem of choosing a topic is considerably simplified. You do not have to "understand Faulkner" or "the causes of the Great Depression" or "the meaning of existence" in order to write a sophomore paper. Begin with whatever interests you, even if it is only a single person, or phrase, or event.

And speaking of stupid, boycott all the Cliff's and Monarch and other shortcuts to an easy C which can be found all too easily in every college bookstore. Many of these can also be found on professors' bookshelves. We read them too. Some of us (God forgive us) write them. At the very least, we eventually come to recognize key sentences from them from the many times innocent undergraduates have repeated them. I even had one lame-brain student list the Monarch Notes edition of a text in his bibliography.

The biggest problem with these notes is not that they save you from having to work or even think, but that they are altogether simple-minded when not outright wrong. They are written for consensus. That is, they represent the lowest common denominator of opinion about any given text, and that is pretty low. Their generalities are about as insipid as you can get for the simple reason that any opinion we academics all agree on has to be pretty vague. Think of a politician who has managed to run for president offending neither the AFL-CIO nor the *Wall Street Journal*, neither Louis Farrakhan nor the ACLU, neither the right-to-lifers nor NOW? This person may have no enemies, but he or she is not going to have any friends either. When I teach *Moby Dick*, after spending considerable effort unveiling many of the complex layers of significance in the chapter titled "The Whiteness of the Whale," if I have any time left at the end of class I read the banal comments found in one of the standard cribnotes. Most of the students get the point.

Brainstorming

Whether you have no idea or even if you begin with a good idea, the very act of writing can itself somehow be a liberating process. It can open the dams in the mind. Psychiatrists often recommend to their patients who are blocking that they try writing out their thoughts because they know that this often helps break up those dams. Ideas occur to the writer that would not occur if he or she were not already pouring words onto the page. One idea stimulates another in a stream of association that reaches deep into consciousness. A trickle of words soon erodes the levee, and before you realize it the Mississippi is pouring through.

Try scribbling across a blank page any impressions, ideas, arguments, irritations, anything that comes to mind in a frenzy of free association. This process is called "brainstorming" and is the way many successful students come up with their paper topics. Discuss the assignment with friends, enemies, random people you run into in the dorm, your stuffed armadillo, your pet porcupine, even your family. My own best ideas have arisen in opposition to what I have heard others say. Listening to others can be a great aid in helping you define your own take on the subject. Read or listen to the opinion of someone you are sure to disagree with. Go to the library and check out a book report, journal article, or newspaper column on the issue. You may be surprised how quickly responses crystalize in your mind. You may also be surprised by what other readers think is going on. What you at first thought an obvious and commonplace observation may well turn out to be a unique and brilliant insight all your own.

Even if you still have no ideas to scribble out, starting a first draft may be a good way to get an idea. Start not with a topic or idea for you have none. Start instead with a literal description of the subject or one of the characters or the question of the assignment. Since you need to begin with the literal anyhow, try writing a brief summary, in your own words, of the plot or structure of the text. That very act may be all you need to start your mind expanding. Is the text interesting? Do you care about anything or anyone in it? Do you like one character and dislike another? Why? Is that what the author intended? Why? What does this tell you about the author and about yourself? What about the ending? Is it convincing? Is it even an ending? Keep fishing around like this until you feel yourself reacting with an opinion or until you can imagine an opinion whether you are sure if you share it or not. But under no circumstances try to hand in the wandering thoughts of this first draft as if it were a finished essay.

The "Deep Inner Meaning" Debate

Once upon a time, way way back when, literature teachers used to concentrate on the biographical details of the lives of the great authors and discuss in broad, general terms how their ideals furthered the values and visions of the nation. This approach remained basically unchanged and unchallenged until the turn of the century ushered in the literary rebellion of the 'teens and the cultural rebellion of the 1920s. Soon, literary critics, smitten by the fads of Freudianism and primitivism, began looking for phallic symbols everywhere. Others, striving to escape from the tired old glorification of American virtues, took to championing cynical doubters and cultural critics. It was in the twenties, for instance, that Melville was discovered. Then in the 1930s, with the collapse of the economy in the Great Depression, literary critics, like intellectuals everywhere, put their shoulders to the wheel of socialist realism and praised books that enhanced the class struggle.

In the 1940s and 1950s, a group of scholars, wearied to tears by all that pompous, pro-American "literary history" of the last century and the politically relevant socialism of the 1930s, began to insist that close readings of the text alone ought to be the scholar's concern and not nationalism or politics. These "New Critics," as they were called, judged the texts under their scrutiny for internal thematic organization, which they called "unity," and for internal paradoxes, subtle allusions, and verbal nuance. Rejecting historical approaches, they took up the battle cry that a text was a text and only the text itself mattered, that it should make no difference to the reader if it were written in China before Christ or yesterday in the Bronx. Literary and historical studies owe to these New Critics considerable credit for rescuing us from the painful platitudes of political generalities and for returning us to a renewed attention to the subtle internal details of the text. The New Critics may have rejected the old tradition of bringing external ideas to the text, but they more than made up for it by finding profound depths of meaning between the lines of the texts. Students have them to blame for the mind-numbing search for some secret, hidden, "deep inner meaning" that all too often seems to be what college professors are asking for.

But in the 1960s, relevance returned with reawakened passion. No longer the tool of stuffy old literary historians or dogmatic socialists, concern for relevance and for historical context returned history and biography to the study of literature with a new sense of purpose. Interest in the political origins of texts and the political consequences of the images and ideas they presented brought back an interest in the circumstances surrounding the texts. Suddenly it mattered considerably if an author were white or black, male or female, WASP or Asian, gay or straight, rich or poor.

As a result of this move from text back to context, students began to have a choice. No longer restricted to discovering the one great secret TRUTH that the text "means" or that the author intended, students began to explore different approaches to talking about texts. They could take a New Critical approach and look for deeper meaning solely within any given text if they wanted to, or they could examine some of the circumstances of the writing of the text, or they could analyze their own or others' reading of the text. My own discipline of American Studies arose in opposition to the New Critics with a determination to return the recently enshrined text back to its worldly context.

Today, we have gotten so far away from the New Critics that the text itself is often abandoned in critical analysis or at least lost against the back-ground of gender and racial politics. Indeed, to some of my fellow refugees from Woodstock, still personning the barricades of Birmingham, race and gender are all that matter and the study of a text becomes an excuse for political sermons on the sins of the world. Just as some New Critics went too far away from context into the text, some professors today tend to go too far away from the text into the context. But the best scholars, then and now, look at both text and context and tie the internal dynamics of the text to their broader cultural and political significance. And there is a good reason for this.

Putting The Text In Context

Years ago there was a musical comedy about a girl in a circus who fell in love with the puppets but hated the puppeteer. She was a bit confused, and it took the whole damn play and a lot of noisy songs before she figured out that the puppets were in fact aspects of the man she thought she hated. Eventually, she learned to love the man too.

Being a child of the sixties, I never could sympathize with that girl or her problem, and I have an equally hard time sympathizing with any New Critics who write about a book or a poem as if the book or the poem were worlds unto themselves and not extensions of some author who in turn is part of some larger historical and cultural context. Even history texts exist as acts of some historian's imagination. Certainly, all texts have to be dealt with on their own terms, and we need to avoid the tyranny of believing the author's intention the only interpretation possible, but to ignore the puppeteer who is making the characters talk is naive. One can ask why a certain character in a book does something. But one can also push the analysis back a step and ask why the author makes that character act that way. And one can then go a step further and ask what it is that makes that author make that character act that way. The title-page that shows the original publication date is one of the most important pages in any book. That Longfellow's "Midnight Ride of Paul Revere" was written in 1861 suggests that the poem may have more to do with the politics of the Civil War than the mythology of the Revolution.

Thirty years ago the New Critics argued that context is irrelevant and should be ignored, that a poem should be appreciated entirely for its own sake and that it should not matter who wrote it, or when, or why. Today this view seems, shall we say, quaint. Textual voices are extensions of human voices which are themselves extensions of ideologies, races, genders, religions, and all the other interest groups which constitute culture. William Faulkner once said in response to a question that he had no responsibility for what the characters in his books did or said. But he was drunk at the time. In response to outraged critics of *The Awakening*, Kate Chopin said that she "never dreamed of Mrs. Pontellier making such a mess of things" and that by the time she found out "what she was up to" it was too late. I have no idea what her excuse was for such evasive nonsense.

So when you are trying to think of something to write about, be sure to lift your eyes from the page. If you can think of nothing to say about the book, think about the way in which people or problems are presented in the book. Are the ways in which different people are represented fair? Are the presentations stereotypes or are they believable? Even if unfair and unbeliev-able, are they nonetheless compelling? Why? Think about the context of the writing of the book. Why did Harriet Beecher Stowe make Uncle Tom so good and noble? Who was her audience? Was she effective? Is she still? Tom's nobility may have meant one thing to her white audience in the 1850s and other things to other audiences later. How has the context changed and how does that change our appreciation of the book today? Remember also that the main character, or the most noble character, need not be an extension of the author. Indeed, the author may have put no one in the book except characters he or she hated. Do not assume that the voice of the work is the true voice of the author. Writers, as I hope you realize by now, often fake it.

Being one of those people who think in pictures, I like to think of this problem as a series of concentric rings:

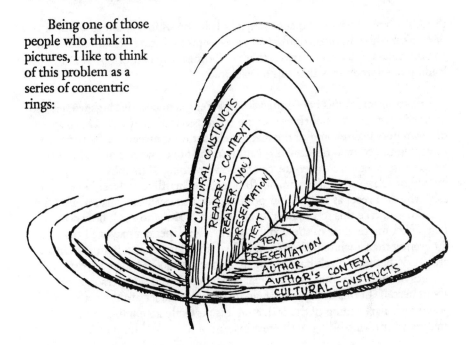

The circle in the middle of the bull's-eye is the text, either the book, or the phrase, or the action or object or personality under study. The first circle around it is the presentation of the object, how it is depicted, both what the author may have intended and how the presentation actually appears to the reader. These may after all be quite different. The next circle then is the author. Who is the person who created these images and stories? Does knowing the author help us to understand why the characters or events are presented as they are? This leads to the next circle which is the author's immediate context. Just as we ask who the author is to get an idea of why the text appears as it does, so we can ask about the author's own personal context to get an idea of why he or she writes as he or she does. Around that circle, then, is the larger worldview or structure within which the author's context needs to be understood, the culture, nationality, class, or whatever other historical contingency shaped that author's life. Beyond that is the cosmic background.

For instance, to understand something in *Uncle Tom's Cabin*, we might simply look at Uncle Tom and ask why he is so good; or we might expand to the first circle and ask why Harriet Beecher Stowe made Uncle Tom so Christlike; or we might continue this expansion and ask who Stowe was, what she believed and why. This might lead us to a discussion of her role as a daughter rebelling against a patriarchal father or to the Romantic rebellion against Calvinism in Victorian American culture. In either case, we might then ask about the role of blacks as symbols in the white American mind, a discussion which in turn could open up the whole concept of symbolic consciousness. For every answer, there is another why that can be asked leading to another level that can be explored.

Cutting across this two-dimensional series of concentric rings we need to imagine another series of rings coming up at us out of the page. This becomes our own personal reading of the text which is still in the center. Rather than exploring the context of Stowe's creation of the novel, we might find it more interesting to explore the context of our own reading of the novel. Thus, instead of asking why Stowe made Tom such a Christlike sufferer, you might ask "why do I react as I do, either positively or negatively, to this image?" And you can also take this to the next level and ask, "OK, who am I, how does who I am affect my reading of the text?" Hence, a black person may well respond differently than a white person, or a male than a female, or a Baptist than an atheist. Whether a black Baptist female is more attracted by the Christian themes or more repulsed by the racial images could tell that person a lot about herself. In this new series of circles, you the reader are the author of your particular reading of the text. And it is perfectly acceptable for you to analyze your own reading of the text instead of Stowe's writing of it.

Although such personal readings are in fact very much the thing these days, there are those who object to this approach as being far too subjective. In deference to them, and to prevent your essay from losing sight of the text in some polemic about slavery or racism or the need for all sinners to be born again, it is a good idea to keep the text in view and to keep your interpretation of even your own responses orbiting around it.

Searching For Symbols

"When correctly viewed," sang Tom Lehrer, "everything is lewd," and anyone who has ever laughed at a dirty joke knows that language is full of double meanings with symbolic reference. Indeed, we are ourselves all symbols and everything around us radiates with symbolic meaning. Colors, shapes, images, sounds, smells, all sensory experience, stimulates associations and memories. These thoroughly subjective impressions and fleeting associations are what we are talking about when we talk about symbols. Even if we are not conscious of the associations in the backs of our minds that attract us and repel us, those unconscious symbolic meanings are there. As Emily Dickinson said, "'Tis not revelation that awaits but our unfurnished eyes." Behind the literal surface, meanings lurk everywhere if only we have the eyes to see them. When John Wayne Bobbitt's Latin American wife cut off his penis with a carving knife, the macho image of America that John Wayne once personified suffered its final blow. It was a powerfully symbolic moment.

The great symbol maker who is always busy, busy, busy behind the scenes had done it again.

What, after all, is a tie? Why do men wear a piece of cloth around their necks? Is it to hide the buttons? What is the symbolic meaning of a tie? Ties are first of all masculine objects; men wear them. They are also symbols of authority, which is a form of power. World leaders, lawyers, businessmen, men who expect to be taken seriously all wear them. So ties are long narrow objects that hang down in the middle of men's bodies that are symbols of masculine power. They tend to be pointed too. Those flat, cut off ties can be found in the backs of the racks, but they are clearly less popular. Maybe John Bobbitt wears one. And what about bow ties? Aren't they usually associated with a Mr. Peeper's nerdy wimpiness? You get the idea.

In Slovakia, where I labored for a year trying to bring American culture to the recently liberated victims of a socially-constructed utopia, I was startled to learn that on the morning after Easter, men and boys carrying home-made whips traditionally visit the homes of women. When the females open the door, the males whip them across the back and then throw perfumed water on them. Then the females, to make the symbolic game complete, hand the guys Easter eggs. And as if that isn't bad enough, the mothers then reward the guys for symbolically impregnating their daughters by handing out candy to the kids and booze to the older guys. When I suggested that this ritual had obvious sexual symbolism, my Slovakian students were outraged. "You decadent Westerners see sex everywhere," I was told. I couldn't deny it. But when asked what the ritual meant, the students told me they did it because their ancestors did it. And why did their ancestors do it, I asked? Because their ancestors before them did it; that's why! They were not ready to admit that this ritual might have arisen with symbolic meanings since lost in the fog of time and kept alive by the enduring power of that unconscious symbolism. They clung to the literal.

Our clothes and our rituals are thus full of symbolic meaning, and so are our words and texts. We all recognize status symbols like expensive cars and LA Gear Newlights. What about the many ways different groups try to make themselves look cool: the grunge look, the prep look, the corn-row hair, dreadlocks? Whether intentional or unintentional these are all symbols. They all have unspoken meanings. So do the clothes, the words, the actions of persons in texts and in history. Finding symbolic meanings is simply a matter of seeing beyond the literal and being willing to let one's imagination run free. Think of your text as one of those Holusion posters they sell in the malls in which, after you gaze cross-eyed for a few minutes, the surface pattern dissolves to reveal an open window onto a previously unseen world beyond. Sometimes, symbolic meanings seem to be revealed to us; more often, we bring our own interpretations to them.

Sticking to the traditional meanings that have historically been associated with traditional symbols can even get you into trouble. Recently, the African-American novelist Alice Walker was named a California "state treasure" and presented with a sculpture of a nude woman's torso. Those presenting the award saw this plaster Venus as a symbol of classical art. Walker, who had just written a book on female mutilation, was outraged at what she saw as "a decapitated, armless, legless woman, on which my name hung from a chain." Such figures may symbolize art to some, she said, but to her they symbolize "domination, violence, and destruction." After insulting the people who sought to award her, Walker decided to keep the award, but she keeps it in a box.

When an author comes right out and tells you that a necklace is "like" a slave's chain or that a tie is "like" a penis, we call that a simile: this is "like" that. When the author never makes the symbolic meaning explicit but throws out clues and hints, we call that metaphor. In Ken Kesey's *One Flew Over the Cuckoo's Nest*, Randall P. McMurphy gives up his life to liberate his friends. Even without the electrodes placed on his head like a "crown of thorns" or the table shaped like a cross or the twelve disciples who go fishing with him, we recognize McMurphy as a Christ symbol and his death as an extended metaphor for the crucifixion.

Nor are we restricted to the symbolic meanings intentionally stuck in by some author; writers themselves do not always know why they do what they do. That is why critics can get away with saying that a text is really all about something else of which the author had nary a clue. Is the hunt for the great White Whale really all about addiction to cocaine? Is Madonna really a symbol of piety and not sacrilege? Who knows? Indulge your suspicions. Follow the clues and see where they lead.

That was what Charles Manson did. Whatever may be said about his or his followers' murderous deeds, Manson's interpretation of the Beatles' "White Album" in terms of the Book of Revelations and the racial politics of the 1960s was brilliant. Had he been an English professor at Berkeley, they would have awarded him tenure, a different sort of life sentence than the one he now serves. Manson clearly understood that the imagination needs to leave the literal behind. "The original sin," he said, "was to write it down." Nor was he tied by any narrow adherence to authorial intent. When asked if the Beatles really intended all that he read into their lyrics, his response was as modern as the latest lit-crit theory: "I don't know whether they did or not. But it's there. It's an association in the subconscious. This music is bringing on the revolution, the unorganized overthrow of the Establishment. The Beatles know in the sense that the subconscious knows."

The other lesson of the Manson example is one you already know, that following the threads of one's imagination into the labyrinth of the mind might lead not to the promised land but into the bottomless pit. The wilderness of ideas can be both an exciting and a dangerous place. There are definitely risks there. But if we bravely face the risks, and avoid the pit that Manson fell into, we might even be among those who cross the frontier and break on through to Canaan.

Cynics And Essentialists

Knowing something about one of the current academic debates can help you approach the problem of finding a topic in ways that will impress your grader. These debates are nothing new, but every generation reinvents the wheel and calls it by a new name. Keeping up with the language of criticism, knowing which trendy words to use, is important. The successful academic lives off the fad of the land.

Texts, whether history or literature or works of art, can be approached as if they came loaded with their own inherent significance or as if they were artful manipulations for some ulterior end. Those who believe in the ultimate importance of the intention of the author, or the meaning of the work, or the eternal beauty of a work of art are called "essentialists." Theirs is the classic position of the romantic, believing in some ultimate truth which can be found, some God within, some true meaning really present in the text. On the personal, psychological level, essentialists are romantics who believe that there is a true self deep within each human person waiting to be found.

Cynics, on the other hand, tend to believe that such readings of texts are much too innocent. They claim that there is no transcendent absolute but only a world of shifting allegiances and interests. The Constitution, they say, was not a "miracle at Philadelphia," but the worldly compromise of a group of self-interested politicians trying to figure out a way to keep their friends and fortunes on top. Beauty, they say, is an emotional reaction in the eye of the beholder which is dependent upon the beholder's needs and wants. "Love" is a glandular condition. The self is a socially constructed illusion, a product of the conservative forces that hold society together and shape each new person to a standard mold. These hardened spirits believe there is no spirit, no essential truth behind the veil, only the endless materialist bumping together of random atoms. Thus, to them everything is relative: there is no such thing as Truth, but different people of different social groups, genders, religions, and classes will see different things and call them true.

Essentialists approach a text looking for some inherent truth and beauty; the cynics approach the same text asking how it was constructed, by whom, and why. Take either approach, but be prepared to defend yourself from the other side. Read the text, or consider the assignment. If you can't find some

intrinsic meaning or beauty which you want to discuss, then take a construc-
tionist view and ask as Cicero did in the Roman Senate, "Cui Bono," to whom
the good? Who benefits? Who loses? Why is this text constructed the way it
is? Why do people respond to it as they do?

Many texts, especially in American literature, deal with this very theme of
whether the self is to be found in the social constructions of civilization along
the shore or in the lonely depths of the soul on a raft adrift down the Mississippi. Should Edna Pontellier have sought for meaning at home among her
friends and family? Or was she heroically escaping the structural cage in order
to find some essential freedom when she stripped naked and swam into the
depths of the sea? What about Thelma and Louise? If you can understand
this debate and apply it to the text, whether the author invites you to or not,
you should do well on any college paper.

Before Plunging In

A word of caution is in order here.

Once you have a rough idea of what you want to write about, you might
want to reconsider before you commit yourself. One of the most crucial
decisions is here being made, and too precipitous a jump might land you in
trouble.

When I graduated from high school, not wanting to rush right into
college, I served for a year on a tramp steamer that travelled the American
coast and the South Pacific. Coming back from Panama, we stopped in
Charleston Bay for a customs inspection. One of the things the inspectors
were looking for was dope. The other crew members were wise to this dance.
Seeing that I was the only white gringo among the crew, they figured my
room would be the last one to be searched. So they decided to hide their stash
with me. But when it came to finding a hiding place, they had a rule: Reject
the first ten places you think of, even if some of them seem foolproof. The
idea was that if we thought of them, so would the inspectors. There was a
deliberate rejection of the arrogant assumption that somehow any idea that
popped into our heads would not just as easily pop into anyone else's. It was
good advice. And the eleventh hiding place was a beaut. As it happened, the
inspectors looked into my doorway, saw that I was white, nodded politely to
me, and then ransacked the other rooms. Since they never entered my room,
we never found out if our hiding place was a safe one. Nevertheless, the lesson
stuck with me. And it applies equally well to the writing of college papers.

Any idea that pops into your head is bound to pop into the heads of
almost every other person in the class. There is no such thing as "free will"
(see my essay in *Harvard Theological Review* on Jonathan Edwards and B.F.

Skinner). We are all products of our environment and our genes. Our differences are due to different contingencies of reinforcement. Our thoughts are not created by us. They come irresistibly out of the depths of the mind. We cannot cause a thought to come before we have already thought it; nor can we stop a thought from coming without first thinking it. Ideas are like other sensations that are perceived by the mind. Just as we hear sounds and see sights, we "feel" thoughts. But for some reason, we are cursed with the arrogant illusion that we somehow create our thoughts. Not so.

Hence, you want to avoid jumping on the first idea that pops into your head. Since you are quite similar to your fellow students and since you are all in the same classroom environment, the chance of the same ideas being created in all of your minds is very likely. And sure enough, most papers on any given topic in any one class bear a remarkable and boring similarity. The few papers that are different stand out. They wake us up. They impress us. We say, "Here is a student who can think and not just react like some Pavlovian dog." In fact, such students are also reacting, but they are reacting from a more complex level and will get better grades.

CHAPTER 3
Choosing A Voice

Writing In Your Own Voice

Part of the choice you have to make when you choose a topic is the voice in which the paper is to be written. Voices are extensions of people and like people they have different viewpoints and opinions. None is objective. Thus the topic of your paper will be closely related to the voice in which you choose to write. Too many students take for granted that any college paper has to be in a pompous professorial objective voice. This is a mistake. Some professors go to great lengths to stress the importance of writing in your own voice. This is good advice, but it can be a bit simplistic. Most of us, after all, have several different voices. We speak one way to our peers, another way to our boyfriends or girlfriends, and a different way altogether to authority figures. Which one is truly us?

Despite what you may have heard in the schoolyard, very few of us teachers really want to see students assume our voices and regurgitate our words back at us. When we do get such papers, we carefully turn the pages with rubber gloves and breathe through our mouths to avoid the smell. We are embarrassed. We might sigh and tell ourselves that at least the student was paying attention, and in a well-crafted paper in a well-ventilated room that might be worth a B. But it is not what we want. We really want each student to draw upon his or her own reading, thinking, experience, and insights and to show us something we have not yet seen. We want our students to use the paper as an opportunity to say what they have to say, to tell their own truths. We want you to teach us something we do not already know.

For this reason, I used to be one of those teachers who require their students to tell the truth, to speak in their own most honest voice, to say what they really believed about the subject under consideration and not even think about what they thought I wanted them to believe. It became apparent, however, that in saying all this, important and true as it was, I was burdening them with the additional responsibility of trying to figure out who they were and what they believed before they could even begin to write the simplest sophomore paper. To make the resolution of the adolescent identity crisis a prerequisite for writing a paper is indeed throwing an all but insurmountable obstacle into the path of the earnest undergraduate. Many students stumble at the threshold unable to write a word because they haven't the vaguest idea either what they are "supposed" to say or what they personally want to say.

Adopting Other Voices

So instead I now suggest to my students: if you are unsure of yourself, then be someone else. Be yourselves if you can, but if you are not able to come up with a good topic of your own, if you are unsure of your own personal opinion, then choose a voice. Choose a personality. Who would you like to be? If you cannot come up with a clear idea of what you think about *Moby Dick*, then think about what a Trotskyite lesbian terrorist gang leader might think, or a capitalist banker, or Donald Trump, or Jesse Jackson, or Hillary Clinton, or your football coach, or your Yiddish uncle, or one of the characters in the text, anyone but your teacher. The exasperated-Professor-voice of this booklet is a good example; in reality, I'm what my friend Karen Fuog calls a "wuss," a softy, really! I sound strict, but I give more As than I ought to admit.

As a way of introducing this possibility, when I teach composition I ask my students to write a paper describing their most admired relative. Their next paper has to be in the voice of that relative. It is more an exercise in acting than in honesty, but, hell, as Shakespeare said, we are all acting our parts upon the stage anyhow. Sincerity is for saints and mystics, or for liars. Besides, I don't know who you "really" are any more than you do. All I want is a clearly identifiable voice with a distinct opinion backed up by some facts as evidence for your argument. Indeed, I also want to be entertained. Don't bore me; entertain me. Ham it up.

The reason for asking for honesty in the first place is not, I confess, because I care all that much about your personal psychological development. I primarily want to read a paper that struts the solid certainty of an honest heartfelt opinion. It is the good, solid feeling that goes with conviction that I want, even if it isn't true. The best works of literature may well be brilliant deceptions, as all human endeavors must ultimately be. "All is vanity" said the prophet, and he was right. If you are one of those lucky self-deceived souls who thinks he or she knows something, then good, go for it. Use "your" own most honest voice. But if you are still in the wilderness of youthful uncer-tainty, then "choose a voice." If you have to, fake it.

Sin Boldly!

One important point about your adopted voice and its argument: you have at least to pretend to believe it. Like Solomon and all great minds that ever contemplated the human condition, Martin Luther was right when he said that all of humankind are sinners and sin in every thought and deed and must necessarily sin, so far are we removed from God. His response was, he declared, to "sin boldly." Do not hide quivering under the bed. Do not shuffle shamefully onto the stage full of abject apologies. Be assertive, be bold, adopt a self-confident voice. Fake it if you have to. The constructionists may be right. Our worldly institutions and values may all be relative and artificial constructs. But few of those who believe this line can be found burning the ten dollar bills in their wallets. We live in the world "as if." To some that "if" is a constantly looming threat; to others it's a challenge.

Look at Ronald Reagan. He had no idea what he was talking about. He acted out the part of the self-confident leader and he got himself elected president twice and was a fairly successful president despite himself. The only difference between Harvard students and community college students is that Harvard students think they are right even when they are wrong and community college students think they are wrong even when they are right. The amount of prior knowledge or the ability to think are about the same, believe me. I've been there. The students who get into Harvard are the ones who adopted (or were given along with their trust funds) self-confident voices early in their careers and stuck with them. They are not self-confident because they are smart; they are what we call "smart" because they are self-confident. So be assertive. Don't be a wimp. The columnist George Will is a very good example, most of the time, of a fine essay writer. So is that crypto-fascist Pat Buchanan. Who can forget his description of Republicans deserting Reagan during Irangate as hyenas "heading for the tall grass" or his inflammatory suggestion at the 1992 Republican Convention that "we take back our culture, block by block?" What makes these phrases memorable? Both of these men have clear and definite (if wrong) opinions that provide them with the self-confidence to sin boldly.

So don't quibble and equivocate and hide behind excuses. Don't begin by saying, "In my opinion...," or "It seems to me that..." These give you away. They say, "It's just little old stupid me saying this and it's probably wrong, so don't hit me, please." That kind of cringing only brings out the bully and the sadist in me. I smell fear, and I pounce, pouring red ink like blood all over the page. Instead, sin boldly! Say "Beyond a doubt, Dan Quayle was a communist dupe and an agent of the international communist conspiracy." I know it's you talking; you don't have to tell me. I know it's your opinion; that is obvious. Make the best argument you can backed up by the best evidence and the tightest logic.

Already I can hear what Robert Burns called the "unco' good and the rigidly righteous" bewailing the immorality of such arrogance. I make no apologies. Nor will I claim some higher morality or justifiable excuse for this approach. Biblical prophecy notwithstanding, the meek are not going to inherit the earth, not in this generation, or at least not until the strong are through with it. Besides, sweet reasonableness, more often than not, is a clever disguise for barely concealed self-interest. Writing is a tool of survival and power. As Tom Peters, a management consultant for one of the 80s hot software development firms once told the *Washington Post,* "In order to do anything interesting on this planet, you've got to be insanely arrogant."

Arrogant is probably the right word for it, too. The literary theorists who dominate the academic world in these dark and dangerous times have concluded that everything is socially constructed, that there is no absolute truth. Their hero, Jacques Derrida, is often quoted as having said (albeit in French), "There is nothing outside the text." If this is true, then each of us is a constructed text. Each of us is an act being played upon the stage. There is no TRUTH outside our constructed texts. We are all faking it anyway, so why worry about sincerity, truth, and all those romantic, essentialist heresies? If the "self" is an invented construction, then your own invention is as real as the social construction you grew up with. It may seem insanely arrogant, but go ahead and choose a voice.

As long as you are being, or pretending to be, arrogant, never announce what it is you are going to do; just do it. Jump right in feet first. Don't ever say, "In this paper I am going to show that Dan Quayle may be considered a member of the international communist conspiracy. I am going to make an argument that he did more than any other human to bring about the destruction of the United States by bankrupting the nation in the name of anti-communism. Then I will provide supporting evidence to back up my claim." Such cautious announcements of intent bespeak uncertainty. Instead, simply state your assertion boldly. Then present your argument and your facts. Long-winded introductions are tiresome. They are but doormats. I wipe my feet on them.

The key here is self-confidence, a quality that unfortunately cannot be taught. You need to liberate yourself from the fear of being wrong or the fear of flunking. Students who write careful cautious timid papers in an attempt to appease the anger of the arbitrary red pen of the grader will not do as well as they who angrily or boldly or proudly or insanely throw caution to the wind, damn the torpedoes, and charge bravely ahead. We graders like to be entertained and we like ideas, facts, thoughts. We tend to be those peculiar kinds of people who actually read books for fun, and the kinds of books we like to read are bold and imaginative and original and lively. They are books full of real voices really alive on the page, voices that teach us something or reveal a new angle.

Dissing The Prof

The main problem with the careful, correct paper is not only that it bores us, but that it insults us. Try to put yourselves in your English professor's tweed jacket. You are sitting in just one of his or her three or four courses. In your course alone 38 papers each about five pages long have just been turned in. That's about 190 mind-numbing pages. If each paper is given, say, fifteen minutes to read and correct, that is 570 minutes. Allow 30 minutes here and there to get up, stretch, go to the bathroom, get a beer from the fridge, slop the hogs, you have 600 minutes of reading or ten solid hours. And we are not talking here about a good juicy novel. We are talking about the same thing over and over and over repetitively. It is like eternity in a highway traffic jam, inching along, stopping, inching along, stopping. Add to this the fact that most papers written for English classes sound the same — safe objective third person narratives all done in a pseudo-scholarly imitation of what students think English professors sound like. And that is where the insult comes in.

Parents of small children are always horrified when they first hear their little darlings sounding just like them. It is a massive embarrassment to see themselves suddenly as others see them. "Oh, my God, is that what I sound like? Good Lord, I didn't mean any of that seriously." So with student papers. By writing in a pseudo-English professor voice, students are imitating what they think they hear. They are telling us what we sound like to them. I cringe in horror every time. Surely they didn't learn that from me?

Avoid therefore any attempt to sound the way you think an English paper ought to sound. The results of such efforts are almost invariably pompous and painful. Be true to your own voice, or the voice of your paper, but consider your audience, your readers.

Voices To Avoid

Once you know who you want to pretend to be, another warning is in order. Some voices do not succeed as well as others. Without crushing your creativity, I need to point out that there are political considerations here whether we like them or not. If you insist on using an obnoxious voice, do so in such a way that the voice clearly discredits itself. I emphasize "clearly." The mere fact that a voice is obviously, say, racist does not by itself show that the author understands that it is objectionable. You would not believe some of the things that I have had students write and mean. I am braced for anything, no matter how ugly or bizarre.

Do not, I repeat, <u>do not use sarcasm</u>. That way destruction lies. Students, especially those who often use sarcasm in their daily discussions, find that they cannot resist sarcastic quips and digs. But these rarely work. In fact, they often backfire. The reason is that sarcasm requires tone of voice to communicate its sarcastic intent. And any tone of voice you might imagine as you write your paper is in your head only and not in the words on the page. You might write, "And of course everybody hates uppity women," intending the comment to be read sarcastically, but the reader only sees the words on the page, and he or she may well not read them that way at all. What you read in a sarcastic voice in your own mind might well come across as serious intent to an innocent, objective reader. Even Jonathan Swift's "Modest Proposal," an often anthologized example of successful irony, was taken quite seriously by a horrified few. Communication is difficult enough these days without risking disaster. Most humor, and sarcasm in particular, depends upon the assumption that your readers share your basic worldview and will therefore recognize a statement thoroughly outside of that worldview as sarcasm. It is an unfortunate fact of modern American life that there is no longer, if there ever was, a generally accepted worldview. As Ted Danson can confirm, attempts to be funny don't always work. Avoid sarcasm.

This is particularly true on E-mail. Much of the writing students do these days is on the Internet, where the absence of voice, tone, and facial expression combine with the quickness of response and the shortness of the message to create horrendous failures of communication. Many a simple E-mail message has resulted in flame wars that raged on for days until finally burning themselves out. The use of those cutesy little computer faces, :), are a poor substitute for human presence. Anyone who has spent much time on the Internet knows full well the dangers of sarcasm. Do not say it unless you mean it, for someone somewhere will surely take you at your literal word.

Beware also of the flowery and ornate voice, unless you mean to discredit it. This is perhaps a personal antipathy of my own. But others share it. Much of Mark Twain's *A Connecticut Yankee in King Arthur's Court* is devoted to ridiculing Sir Walter Scott and the idiocies of *Ivanhoe*. Too many students today have spent too much time playing computer variations of Dungeons & Dragons that wallow in the worst sort of a revived, pseudo-medieval Sir Walter Scott verbiage. Gag me with a Grue before even thinking of adopting the voice of any of the characters in King's Quest, even if you're a member of SCA.

Closely related is the kind of political BOMFOG that vomits over the airwaves every election season. BOMFOG is a useful acronym for rhetoric that wanders on eloquently about the "Brotherhood of Man and the Fatherhood of God." Such phrases say nothing while trying to give the impression of being vaguely on one side or the other without having to make any specific commitment.

And speaking of commitment, use the active not the passive voice. During the Iran/Contra scandal, when the Reagan PR machine finally admitted that "mistakes were made," the *Washington Post* ran an editorial noting the curiously evasive use of the passive voice. Who made those mistakes? The politicians were not going to say. Instead, they withdrew like worms back into the mud of the passive voice.

Whatever voice you choose, try to resist the temptation to preach. Moralism makes for lousy papers. For one thing, moral pronouncements tend to assume that a common sense of morality exists and that an appeal to this common morality will be effective. This is often unwarranted. Our most sincerely held beliefs may well be the products of our peculiar environments and not as universal as we wish to believe. If the moral posture is one that is widely accepted, then the point of the paper is quite ordinary and not a good topic. Essays on racism in these delicate times often end up as safe, sane, moralistic pronouncements about how bad hate is and how wonderful it would be if everyone could just get along and love each other. Is this an argument? Who would argue against it?

Such sappy sentimentalisms beg the important questions. Why do some people hate? What causes it? How can these causes be addressed? Can they be addressed? How is bigotry manifested? In what unconscious ways does it make itself felt? How can the heart be changed? What must we do to be saved? These are the kinds of analytical questions that need to be asked and answered. We are all against poverty, war, and injustice, for motherhood and pesticide-free, chemically-uncontaminated apple pie. Accept that and move on. If you suspect that some of us do need a little moral preaching, then the job of your paper is not to preach the word but to show us that our assumptions of innocence are unjustified. The task of making us see the beams in our own eyes is a complex one and requires more than a moralistic finger wagging in our faces.

Imagining Your Audience

This is an important rule, not to be brushed over lightly: you must have in mind an idea of who it is you are writing for. And here again, you must fake it. Of course, the reality is that you are writing your college paper for a single reader, the teacher, moi. But you must pretend otherwise. I usually tell students to pretend that they are writing their English paper for an atomic physicist. This is someone whose intelligence they have to respect but whose knowledge of the subject may be a bit weak. They therefore have to remind her occasionally of just what is going on, but they have to do so gently and respectfully without being patronizing or snide. Even *The Washington Post* in publishing a story about golf will gently remind its readers that the biggest celebrity to attend the match was Danny Quayle, former vice-president of the United States. Chances are that the vast majority of the readers know who Danny Quayle is, but still there is that necessity to remind the occasional absent-minded professor who has been in the lab for the last twelve years.

Ungrammatical Voices

Here one rule quickly crashes against another. What should you do if you choose to write in a colorful voice but capturing that voice requires writing in ungrammatical English? Can writing according to the strict rules of grammar produce anything but bland, boring prose? *Huckleberry Finn* is a good example of a book written in an ungrammatical voice which in fact succeeds very well despite Huck's lack of formal English. Mark Twain took a risk writing that book, but such risk-taking is part of the challenge of writing. Students often complain that I challenge them to be different, to take risks, but that I then give them grief for getting it wrong. And they are right.

A no-man's land exists between the civilized town and the wilderness. This frontier is where the excitement erupts. No one ever crossed that frontier without the risk of being shot full of arrows by the possessors of that disputed turf. What those students were asking me for were risk-free risks. But good writing takes risks, real ones, and good writers have to get used to that. When you take your pen in hand, or when you load up your word-processor program, you are lighting out for the territory with Huck.

A good example would be that of a distinctive regional voice. To write or to speak correctly all too often means to adopt the standardized WASPy style associated with rural Connecticut or perhaps the Pacific Northwest. The speech patterns of Mississippi, white and black, are practically another language. Do we all have to blend into a bland WASP soup? By no means! Diversity and multiculturalism call us to celebrate the cacophony of voices that make up America. Even if the Mississippi voice is ungrammatical, try it and take the risk.

In one of my composition classes, a disgruntled group of students from the South finally found the nerve one day to rebel against my Bostonian convictions. I had corrected several of them for describing someone who was awaiting the arrival of a friend as "waiting on the train." The only person "waiting on a train," I insisted, was the waiter in the dining car. The others were waiting "for" the train. The Southerners fought back insisting that mine was as much a regional colloquialism as theirs and that theirs had at least as much legitimacy. I didn't like it, but fearing secession and another Civil War, I conceded the point.

CHAPTER 4
Shaping Your Argument

Why Must We Argue?

Your voice needs to be making an argument. This doesn't have to be an angry confrontational argument. Nor does it have to be profound. But there does have to be some point to it all, some message your voice is trying to get across. If you cannot imagine anyone disagreeing with what you are saying then your paper is not an argument. A paper saying that the sky looks blue on a sunny day is not an argument. A paper arguing against wife-beating or racism is equally pointless. Who would disagree? You need to go beyond conventional moralisms and say something specific. Argue that alcohol taxes ought to be raised to pay for federally funded women's shelters. That'll get you into an argument in any bar in America.

Presenting and then resolving a conflict is the classic approach to writing any paper. Start off with a problem, or a question, or a mystery. A body lies mutilated in the biology lab; whodunit? Lord Cornbury, one of the colonial governors of New York, used to solicit sailors on the docks while dressed in full drag; why wasn't he ashamed of his behavior? Why can't that wimp Hamlet make up his mind? What complex secrets lie behind the innocent smile of the blonde in the movie? Why is dark always thought of as evil?

Because we live in a cause and effect universe, every aspect of any text, whether historical, or literary, or psychological, contains mysteries waiting to be revealed. Despite the arrogant posturing of academics and scientists, psychologists and economists, human behavior is still a complete mystery. Any activity involving human beings is thus loaded with unanswered and often unspoken questions. All you need to do to come up with an argument is to be as innocent and evil as a child who asks "why?" Remember that every event and statement is an effect and that every effect has a cause. If the reason for an author's or a character's words is not obvious, that is your opportunity to argue for your own interpretation. It is a mystery that needs to be solved.

Having a solution to your mystery, or an answer to your question, at the end of the paper is always helpful, but even that is not necessary. To lay out a problem, to ask penetrating questions, to explore some of the possible answers, to report on other persons' suggested answers can by themselves be worthwhile endeavors. But we teachers do want our students to take risks and to try to express an opinion.

The worst papers tend to be written by students who are afraid to voice an opinion, who are afraid of being wrong. Don't worry about being wrong. It's not you anyhow, it's your voice that is making the argument. Most of the time, I don't even care what you believe. Remember, this is not indoctrination. We are not here to brainwash you into accepting our beliefs. We are here to teach you how to argue persuasively. A paper is not a scantron test; it is an opportunity for you to go beyond the mere recitation of facts and to say something about them. There is enough time for neutrality in the grave. In the meantime, we are creatures of passion, driven by our likes and dislikes, hopes and fears. Do not be afraid to reveal them.

Relativism is the last refuge of the coward. Students who are afraid to voice an opinion, any opinion, hide in the fog of relativistic rhetoric. Once while teaching some provocative poetry to my students in Slovakia, I asked one young man what he thought the words meant. He gave me a literal translation as if we were in first year English. I asked him then what he thought of the poet's idea as stated in the poem. "The poet," he said, "made this statement because it is what he believed. He is saying what he believes because he believes it. That is what I think." I think of that student often. He was brought up in a system in which having personal opinions was considered downright immoral. There was one truth, worked out by the Party, and students were expected to learn it and spit it back. The idea of admitting they had private thoughts, much less speaking them out loud in a public room with an authority present, was frightening to them.

But what excuse do American students have for hiding behind such relativism? Our system insists on each individual's worth. We want to know what the world looks like from each student's unique perspective. We want all the conflicting opinions to be heard and debated. Yet many students believe that democracy is an excuse not to have an opinion. When asked whether a particular statement is right or wrong, these students repeat the democratic belief that everyone is entitled to his or her own opinion and that each person's opinion depends on that person's beliefs. "Yes," I come back at them. "That is true. And what I am asking for is your opinion. Tell us not what is true for everyone else or anyone else; tell us what you personally think."

No Right Or Wrong

Therefore, once again, and it needs to be repeated, don't worry about being "wrong." Being wrong is, at least in the humanities, almost impossible because there are no "right" answers. The academic journals are filled with new and bizarre interpretations of old favorites, and the more bizarre the more likely to get published and to win some clown tenure and a life-time job grading sophomore papers. What we mean when we give a "D" is that there is no real argument or that the argument is illogical or is not supported by evidence or perhaps is inconsistent with other evidence in the text. Sometimes it means that we cannot be sure that you read the right book. The English teacher who asks, "What is the meaning of this poem?" is a fool. There is no one "the meaning." There are interpretations and there are arguments for those interpretations. That is all we really know. All those people who insist that they really know what they are doing are fooling themselves, or you, or both. Only the saints who have heard directly from God know the TRUTH; the rest of us are stuck in the constructed dung heaps of the earth.

Poets themselves love to confess to being "inspired" *ab extra*, from outside themselves. "I is another," said Arthur Rimbaud. Certain words or images were put in poems just because they "felt right," but the poets often are no more certain why than we readers are. They know what they thought they were doing, but something else may have been going on of which they were totally unaware.

No intelligent person can deny the conditional or contingent nature of consciousness. We are shaped by unconscious forces in the environment and the soul. Sometimes it is easier for a stranger to see through our own best rationalizations and expose us even to ourselves. So do not fall into the trap of imagining that there is some hidden "right" answer all the experts secretly agree on. Received opinion is often wrong and usually boring; the text is yours to interpret. It certainly helps to show that you know and understand the conventional wisdom or the professor's own pet theory, but do not be afraid to go beyond it. This is as true for the social sciences; if you don't like the standard Marxist or psychological or feminist analysis, try another or try your own.

Imagine Jesse Jackson and Jesse Helms each writing a history of the Clinton Presidency. Both texts will be histories. But which one is "right" would be pretty much a matter of subjective political perception. Some reviewers will judge the books entirely on the basis of their own prejudices, of course disguising their bias under the illusion of objectivity. Liberals will hail the Jackson history as "inspired," "insightful," and "eloquent" while condemning the Helms history for its narrow ethnocentricity. Conservatives will praise the Helms history for its "penetrating analysis" and "constructive moral perspective" while condemning the Jackson history for being unscholarly and unobjective. All the reviewers will find objective reasons for their subjective opinions, and it is on these that disinterested readers (if there are any) will have to make their own judgements. Thus, each reviewer will try to find fault with the logic, with the evidence, and with the perspective of the text while searching out reasons for praising the text the reviewer is biased toward. We call this scholarship.

Histories written about the dynasties of the kings of England are no different than histories of the dynasty of Bill and Hillary. The older histories seem more objective only because we are no longer party to the passions and debates that shaped the different viewpoints of their politics. But just as there can be a dozen different angles from which to analyze any political event today, so there are dozens of ways in which to look at any historical or psychological or theological or literary event of the past. Even worse, we have to multiply the number of different parties competing then by the number of different lenses through which we can interpret their disputes today. That is why we say in the humanities that there are no right answers, only opinions and arguments in favor of those opinions. Hence, you cannot be wrong in terms of your argument. You can only be judged fairly on the basis of how you argue, how you use evidence, cite sources, draw conclusions, and refute your critics.

Therefore, the bolder the argument, the better the paper has a chance to be. We really are not after you to discover some specific buried message or "deeper meaning" hidden cleverly in the text. We are after you to come up with any interpretation that takes the literal meaning of the text into account and also finds something of interest that is not immediately obvious. Be logical, be informed, be opinionated, back up your points with a lot of facts, evidence, and quotations, and bring in some outside artillery. You can't lose. Only the most bigoted fool of a teacher will nuke you for daring to be different. Such teachers do exist, but they are rarer than you think, and you can go and explain to them that you are really not the crypto-Nazi skinhead whose voice you were assuming in your paper. Note that a certain degree of sensitivity to the sensitivities of us sometimes all-too-sensitive teachers is wise policy.

Daring Dissent

Many students complain to me that their other teachers indeed are such bigots, that they reward students who reflect their views and punish those who are different. On my campus, male students openly chortle over the well-known and successful scenario for acing any course by a feminist. All they have to do, they tell me, is to start off pretending to be macho and sexist and then, over the semester, gradually come over to the point of view of the teacher. The teacher thus rewards them not for their writing but for their "intellectual development" and "heightened maturity." Other students say that to argue a conservative point in a liberal's class, or a liberal point in a conservative's class, is sure death. While I admit that there are some idiotic ideologues on both sides of the political battlefield who do not know or care about the difference between propaganda and education, I suspect that in many of these reported cases, the problem is not one of conforming to the hidden or not-so-hidden agenda of the teacher, but of failing to acknowledge it. All teachers have agendas; make no mistake about that. But most teachers are happy simply to have their viewpoints acknowledged, not digested and regurgitated.

Dissent from the class agenda is probably a healthy response and deserves respect, since it is always harder to resist the current than to go with the flow. But such dissent carries with it the additional responsibility of bowing toward your opponent before the battle starts. All you need do in a brief paragraph near the opening of the paper is to say something like, "Although it is true that Marx predicted the inevitable downfall of capitalism, that the U.S. is a capitalist country which exhibits many of the contradictions Marx discerned in capitalism, and that some of these contradictions can be found in a close reading of our current text, *The Essential Calvin and Hobbes*, nevertheless other forces more than make up for the failings of capitalism and some of these beneficial aspects of American culture can also be found in our text." Then you can go on to make whatever points you originally wanted to.

The real danger with the dissenting paper, and it is one which I have run into numerous times, is the failure to provide any evidence that you have paid attention to any of the class lectures or read any of the texts. That, after all, is a major reason for writing these papers. The grader needs to have some evidence not just of what you believe but that you have done the assigned work. A dissenting argument which never even mentions the class agenda risks being read as an evasion rather than a response. The connection between what you are writing and what was in the assignment may be obvious to you, but you have the responsibility to make it obvious to the grader.

VGs, AEs, And OAs

Many years ago, the *Harvard Crimson* published a guide by a successful student who had mastered the art of passing an exam without studying. "Beating the System," as the essay was called, listed three basic approaches to writing exam essays: the Vague Generality (VG), the Artful Equivocation (AE), and the Overpowering Assumption (OA).

The VG is an easy trap to fall into, but it is to be avoided at all costs. Papers full of VGs are raging seas of confused winds and currents in which the seasick reader prays that the ship will hit a solid rock and bring all the nauseating dizziness to an end. The have no facts, no solid opinions; they paint no pictures. They are like hot, stagnant dinosaur breath. A wonderful Doonesbury cartoon depicts Mike coming into a room where Zonker is writing a term paper. It is full of vague generalities and indirect allusions and BS: "Most problems, like answers, have finite resolutions. The basis for these resolutions contain many of the ambiguities which conditional man daily struggles with. Accordingly, most problematic solutions are fallible." Mike asks, "Which paper is this?" Responds Zonker, "Dunno. I haven't decided yet." Zonker's essay is a good example of a string of VGs. They have no substance, no meat, no facts, and they immediately send a signal to the reader that the writer hasn't a clue.

The AE is a little better, but not much. It at least gives the student who hasn't the vaguest idea what the answer is the opportunity to show what he or she does know. An AE essay usually is full of waffles: "Whether one defines Shelley as a Romantic depends upon a host of complex variables...." An essay on the causes of the Great Depression by someone who didn't get that far in the text might begin, "Before one can hope to understand the causes of the Depression of the 1930s, it is necessary to understand as fully as possible the social conditions of the decade that preceded it." The student can then go on to talk about bathtub gin and flappers, at least giving the grader something to grade, even if it is not the desired answer. AE essays often give themselves away with the use of that TV anchorman all-purpose inanity, "remains to be seen."

The OA, however, is the best approach. This is the equivalent of Luther's "sin boldly." It is simply the assumption of an opinion so bold and imaginative, if totally off the wall, that the reader will be impressed by the sheer daring involved: "The American Civil War was caused, not by slavery or the economics of cotton, but by the North's fear that Southern aristocrats would spread their oppressive institutions into the North and kill the American experiment in freedom." A few facts and a little logic thrown in to back up the OA are all that is needed. Don't worry too much about being "right." Make the best argument you can for the assumption you are pushing. Be bold.

When I was teaching in Czechoslovakia, I was confronted with papers by students who had learned the careful art of saying nothing, and learned it well. Life under Communism had taught them to avoid committing themselves to any ideas, even Marxist ones. You never knew when even the party line might swerve and leave you stranded. So their papers were masterpieces of vague generalities and artful equivocations: "In certain situations, certain events can cause certain repercussions. In such circumstances, it is always best to choose the best solution to the given problems." Zonker had nothing on these kids. But you don't have Communism as an excuse for hiding, and neither do they anymore. Still, sometimes bad habits left over from the tyrannies of our youth maintain their grip on our souls. We must fight against them. We must be bold.

Show What You Know

Knowing that in fact they are really writing for an audience of one, their teacher, some students are tempted to leave out important points or to slide glibly over them with an "as you know," knowing full well since I taught the course that I do know. The problem here is that the purpose of the paper is to help me find out if you know. Therefore, no matter how obvious and repetitious it may seem, you do need to show that you know the basic facts and ideas and definitions. If you repeat a word you heard used several times in class, a generous professor may give you the benefit of the doubt and say, "Well, this student must understand this term in order to have used it." Not me. I have read enough papers by students trying to cover up the fact that they don't even know the title, author, or main character of the book we've been carefully studying for two weeks to have become quite cynical. Show me.

In the development of the paper, you will undoubtedly be using some general terms. These need to be defined. Freedom? Democracy? Racism? Romanticism? Marxism? Structuralism? You may have an idea of what these terms mean, and you may even be right. But what you think they mean may not be what I think they mean. Nor can you safely quote Webster's Dictionary definition at me as if Webster's was handed to Moses on Mount Sinai. I want to know what you think the word means so I can understand your use of it. Such words are notoriously slippery little eels. And far too many students have become adept at throwing around vague and undefined words in such a way that they can write whole papers and never have to know what their own words mean.

Suppose you have been reading a book on psychology or sociology which makes heavy use of the term "repression." On the final exam, your professor asks you something about the word. Or in your final paper, you are required to discuss repression. The first thing you have to do is define the term. You cannot safely open up your Webster's and quote from it. That would be much too easy. Webster's definition may be "right" in some sense, but it may not be what is needed in order to understand the class or the text. You need to go back into your text or your class notes and try to find where it is defined there. You also need to find where it is used and to make sure that the author actually uses it in the way that he or she defined it. Discovering such contradictions may be the hidden puzzle of the assignment. Take nothing for granted.

I have actually used this assignment, and I find that it brings out both the best and the worst in students. After letting the dictionary do their work for them, students outclever themselves in another way by letting the author define the word for them. That is, they go to the place in the text where the word is defined and say something like , "According to author Norman Brown, 'Seperation on the outside is repression on the inside.'" Aside from spelling "separation" wrong, such answers leave it up to me, the reader, to figure out what Brown meant. It provides no clue whatsoever that the student has any idea. Indeed, the suspicion here is that the student is hiding behind the quotations hoping not to have to come out and define the term. Perhaps oral exams are a good idea after all.

Another popular evasion is to use the term but never even try to define it. This works well in speech when, by using a word like "deconstruct" as if we knew what we meant, we force those listening to bear the burden of having to supply the definition. By speaking confidently, we hope to avoid being put on the spot. A gullible professor might overlook this failure to define key terms. But I am not one of those saps, and you cannot count on any of us falling for this trick. Even the sweetest of us have our limits and our down days. In some cases, the initial act of defining the term can be the topic of the entire paper. Let's face it: if you can define abortion as the killing of a human infant, you barely need to go on with any more of the argument. If, on the other hand, you glibly assume that abortion is defined as the taking of a human life, and you go on without having defended that assumption, the rest of your argument will not be worth much.

What works best is clear English speech that is free of complex subtleties or excessive jargon and that sounds like a person talking. A successful definition might be:

Norman Brown defines repression as the action of the rational mind holding down by force, or excluding from consciousness, all of the chaotic emotions of the subconscious. It occurs because the human brain puts a lid on the emotions. It traps them.

Notice how this student moves from a fairly complex statement using undefined psychological terms like "consciousness" to her own more simple language, "It traps them." There is a clear picture here which is communicated from her mind to the reader's mind.

Swindler's List

The opposite of the argument paper is what I call the "list paper." This is the way many of you were taught to write English papers back in high school, and let me tell you, you were swindled. In this model of paper writing, a term paper on "Birds in Shakespeare" might identify three birds in *Macbeth*, four in *King Lear*, and five in *A Midsummer's Night Dream*. The topic sentence points out that there are many different birds referred to in Shakespeare. The birds are then named and located. A particularly ambitious paper of this sort might even say what the birds are doing in relation to the plot or what significance they seem to have. The conclusion announces proudly that therefore we can see Shakespeare's use of birds. There is no argument, no point, nothing, just a list of birds. Who cares? What difference does it make? Who can argue against it? What has anyone learned? Give me a stupid argument over an empty list paper any day! The history paper equivalent of a stupid list paper is a chronological narrative that tells the sequence of events but nothing else: this happened, this happened, this happened, the end. At the very least, explain the order of your list; perhaps a pattern will be revealed that can lead to a meaningful argument. In the social sciences too, interpretation, analysis, significance, insight into causation are the ends desired. We need to know that you know the facts, but we are looking for more than that. With a little imagination, any list paper can be turned into an argument. Everything is controversial these days.

A student of mine from Columbia recently wrote a paper on ethnicity in which he described several of his family's ethnic traits: food, clothing, holiday rituals. It was a well-written paper, and the examples were interesting and lively. But it was basically a list and nothing more. Near the end, he mentioned that his mother sometimes called him a "Gringo" because he had become so American. I suggested that he take that confrontation, put it up front in the topic paragraph, and then reorganize the facts already in the paper around that conflict. He rewrote the paper starting off describing in detail this tension between his family's traditional Columbian lifestyle and his own evolution away from it. He was then able to describe dinners and clothing and language as arenas of cultural conflict. The result was a much better, more meaningful paper, indeed, an A. Everyone likes a good fight.

Also, be sure not only that you have an argument but that you have only one argument. If you have two things to say, write two papers, or make one somehow fit into and under the general umbrella of the more important argument. Think of the whole paper-writing project as the organization of an army going to battle. There can be only one battle plan and one top general. A divided command will produce defeat. Line up all of your battalions in an orderly fashion, face them all in the same direction, and charge.

Battle Tactics

An argument can be thought of as a military maneuver. Once you state your objective in the topic paragraph, you need to begin to move your troops forward. But before you can make your first move, you need to consider your tactics. These will depend largely on your objective and on your opponents. Are you trying to persuade people who already disagree with you? If so, that will require confrontation and refutation. Are you trying to persuade a neutral audience? If so, then you want to be careful not to confront them or you might lose the possibility of winning them over. Much of this depends on the voice you choose and the assumptions you make.

Many arguments fail because the writer makes unwarranted assumptions. If you wish to prove that evolution is a false theory, appeals to the Bible or quotations from fundamentalist ministers might not succeed. You personally might be persuaded by such arguments, but unless your opponent already agrees with you that the Bible is always literally true, you will be resting your argument on an unwarranted assumption, and you will not convince a soul. To avoid this problem, you must either find a common assumption which you can work from, or you must first persuade the reader that the Bible is in fact true. Good luck.

Finding a common ground is a good way to begin your argument. If you can establish a common basis upon which you and your readers agree, then you have a solid base from which to build a persuasive case. We Americans tend to believe that anything natural is good. Thus, analogies from nature are common rhetorical devices. Both feminists and male chauvinists appeal to nature to back up their arguments about the proper relationship between the genders in human society. In the New Testament, Jesus was very fond of analogies, repeatedly comparing difficult concepts to familiar ones: "And why take ye thought for raiment? Consider the lilies of the field how they grow; they toil not, neither do they spin: Yet I say unto you that even Solomon in all his glory was not arrayed like one of these."

Such analogies can be very persuasive, but they can also be very misleading. Before the 1960s, arguments in favor of segregation of the races were also often based upon analogies with nature: different species of birds flock together, don't they? Thus, one needs to consider the assumptions being made even here. Nature isn't always friendly.

Arguments that begin with some common assumption or an analogy with some generally accepted truth are called "inductive." Such arguments begin with some general statement which lead to some specific conclusions. If the reader agrees with the assumption, the argument should prove successful. But in our pluralistic, fragmented world, there are very few, if any, common assumptions left that very many people agree on. And most teachers, if they are any good, can shoot any unproven assumption full of holes. Thus, inductive arguments tend to be less successful than deductive arguments. These are arguments that begin with specifics, with evidence, and then draw general conclusions from that specific evidence.

Be prepared therefore, once you have stated the point you want to establish, to be able to present evidence to back up your claim. The more evidence you can bring up to the front, and the greater variety of evidence you can muster, the better your chance will be of carrying the field. Begin with a proposition or a question or a challenge. Define any potentially questionable terms you might need to use. Then bring in the evidence with which to prove your point. Do not assume that a mere stating of the case is sufficient. Evidence that seems clear to you may seem irrelevant to your reader. You must explain logically how that evidence supports your claim.

This evidence must also be made up of facts, not opinion. We define facts as statements which can be verified by outside observers. Even this is subjective, of course. The *Washington Post* requires three independent verifications before it declares a statement to be a fact; the *New York Times* requires five. You may believe that Jesus rose from the dead, but it is not a fact unless it can be proven by outside evidence. Quotes from the Bible, the book in which this claim is made, cannot be considered as outside evidence.

Keep Your Argument Grounded

Assuming that your topic paragraph stated the argument which you intend to prove, you then in the second and subsequent paragraphs need to lay out the evidence in some logical order. You want your reader to be able to follow you. So begin at a basic level at which there can be little disagreement and take your reader by the hand up the narrow trail to the heights. Do not try to write the entire paper from the heights, but don't stay stuck on the ground either. In other words, begin with the literal and work your way to the profound, returning briefly at the end to the rock from which you started.

This is an important tactic to master. Some students, whether answering in class, scribbling exam essays, or writing term papers, jump instantly to the lofty mountain tops of cosmic generality leaving us earthbound clods breathless and a bit confused. Other students are mere earthworms and never lift their heads out of the soil at all. You need both: the solid earth on which we stand and the enlightened vision which we imagine separates us from the apes and ennobles us. Therefore, begin with literal facts. Begin with some solid rock from the text, some person or quotation or perhaps with some personal experience or reaction of your own. Then slowly ascend through the circles of interpretation making sure that your reader is with you each step of the way. If you are reading *One Flew Over the Cuckoo's Nest* and you want to denounce Ken Kesey's sexism, begin by describing the examples. Then describe your reaction. Then begin to analyze the causes both of his unbearable sexism and of your angry reaction. If you are assigned a cultural study of Easter rituals, begin with your own family's experience. But then ascend from your egg hunting to larger questions: Why eggs? Why do we hide them? What do eggs and chocolate bunnies have to do with the resurrection of Christ? Does anyone really know? If not, if we perform rituals we cannot explain, what does that say about us? Begin with the specific event, ask "why" often enough, and your paper will soon be soaring through the heavens.

Include Objections

Once you have presented your evidence and explained carefully how that evidence proves the point you are trying to make, you then need to take some time to refute objections. After you have shot off your biggest guns, the enemy will still counterattack. You need to be prepared to counter those counterattacks. Include within your paper the objections that have been or might be raised to your argument. Try to imagine the questions that will arise in the mind of the reader. Show that you understand those questions, that you have carefully considered them, and that you have the facts and the arguments to refute them.

A paper defending abortion will have no success as an argument if it fails to acknowledge the position of those on the other side of the debate who believe that a fetus is a human being and that abortion therefore is murder. Say whatever you want about a woman's right to control her own body; as long as the reader believes that abortion is murder, your argument will fall on deaf ears and your paper will fail. Likewise, a paper attacking abortion as murder needs to do more than repeat that claim. The author must try to understand the reasoning of the other side and then show where and why it is wrong.

If you cannot think of any opposing position, then you are in trouble for what you have is not an argument. If you do have an argument but are ignorant of the opposition's views, your defense will be weak. If you know the opposition's views but do not clearly understand them, then you need to do more research and apply more thought.

It is always a good idea to concede some territory to your opponents. No position is 100% right or 100% wrong; we are all sinners fumbling in the dark. Conceding that your opponent may have a point here or there will not weaken your defenses. If nothing else, this tends to disarm them. Absolute positions that refuse to yield an inch create absolute oppositions which are equally stubborn. Surprise your readers. Be reasonable, be understanding, be sympathetic to their concerns, and then when their defenses are down, zap them with logic and club them to death with facts!

CHAPTER 5
How To Lose Your Argument

Unfortunately, it is easier to be critical than to be constructive. It is easier to point out mistakes than to explain how to get it right in the first place. Perhaps this is because human history is a rubble pile of mistakes waiting to be repeated and the right answers are still a promised land somewhere over the rainbow. Whatever the reason, mistakes are easily identified and labelled. You therefore need to be able to recognize some of the most familiar logical fallacies so that you can get to them and correct them before I do.

⟳ Circular Reasoning

Circular reasoning is so prevalent that it even has its own marginal notation. Indeed, its popularity is such that I feel impelled to say something about it: DON'T DO IT!

In case you don't recognize this problem, it is the tendency to explain something by the thing explained. I have had students write on papers that "People like beef because it tastes good." This is circular. Saying they like it and saying that it tastes good are simply two ways of saying the same thing. Thus, the steak's tasting good is not the cause of their liking it. In my early American class, every year someone writes that Emerson was a romantic because he lived in a romantic era. Yes, and it was a "romantic era" because romantics like Emerson lived in it. Which came first? The era or the writers in it? This too is circular reasoning. In almost any discipline, we want you to see beyond the immediate fact to the cause of the phenomena, be it an economic, historical, or literary problem. We live in a cause and effect universe. Accept the terrible truth that things do not cause themselves. In our determined world events have causes. We expect you to search outside of the events for whatever you think might have caused them. I once heard a scholar say, "Our condition is due to the condition our condition is in." My primary response was to wonder why she was being so evasive.

Just Say No To "Just"

It is to emphasize this point that I forbid the use of the J-word, "just," in any of my classes. Nothing "just" happens. Everything has a cause. Saying that something "just" happens is saying in effect that it happens without a cause. This is the kind of sloppiness that we indulge in when we don't think.

However difficult and at times painful, we must fight our way through the tangle to the causes. We must rattle the bars of the prison of our contingency. That is what education is for.

As a generally instructive way of illustrating this problem, I ask my students to tell me what their favorite flavor of ice-cream is. Some say chocolate, some strawberry, some coffee, some octopus kumquat. Some claim not to like ice-cream at all. Others get evasive and deny having any favorites preferring, they say, to make up their own free will when they get into the store. Hah!

Then, having pried some sort of answer out of each student, I go back around the room asking "why." In the first round, a depressingly large number of students say, "I just do," or "it tastes good." Unwilling to let sleeping evasions lie, I keep pushing. Why does it taste good? Why does Jill over here like chocolate and Hans over there like strawberry? What are the factors that produce these differences?

A few logical positivists always fight valiantly for the illusion of free will. "Nothing forces me to choose," they say. "I make up my own mind. I am not influenced by outside factors. I am free to do what I want." But why, I respond, do you want what you want? What produces that wanting? Imagine yourself standing in front of the Baskin-Robbins counter tasting each flavor in your mind. One of them rings a louder bell in memory than others. Or perhaps you want to taste something new and different. Why do some people want to explore and experiment while others stick to the same old same-old every time? We are all free to choose what we want, but the devil is in the wanting which precedes the choice.

This is why little kids dragged into an ice-cream store for the first time stand there in utter confusion and are unable to make up thei. minds. Their well-meaning parents try to be patient, but they cannot understand why Johnny can't make a choice. After all, 38 wonderful flavors beckon. But Johnny has no idea what any of them taste like. He has no memory to call upon. Once he has had some experience, then he will settle on a favorite.

The causes of this choice, or any choice for that matter, carry us deep into the swamp of human consciousness. All of the mysteries of human behavior suddenly come into play. Are our likes and dislikes determined by chemistry? Perhaps the caffeine in chocolate or coffee stimulates receptors in the brain. Maybe our first taste of strawberry ice-cream occurred on a warm day in April when the world was, as the poet said, "puddle wonderful." So the cozy memories of childhood grace became associated with the flavor of strawberry until the taste experience on the tongue conjured up some faint memory of that moment with every bite. The Marxists, no doubt, can tie ice-cream preference to economic and power relationships, and the race and gender folk are working on tieing their concerns to the problem.

Nothing "just" happens. Push your regression back to Adam and Eve and you still have to explain how they got there. Even the Big Bang had to be preceded by something. Some people fill the preceding void with the word "God." Others just scratch their heads. Sorry about that.

Post Hoc, Ergo Propter Hoc

This phrase is Latin for "After this, therefore because of this." We see this logical fallacy used in politics in every administration. The folks in power take credit for everything good that happens; the opposition blames them for everything bad. The recession was George Bush's fault. The Los Angeles earthquake was Clinton's. Because some events occur at the same time as or right after some other event, there is a temptation to assume cause and effect. We call the results of this behavior superstition. Depending upon superstitious circumstance to bolster your argument could be a fatal mistake.

Ad Hominem

Ad Hominem attacks are attacks against people as a means of discrediting their ideas. Basically, it is a weaselly, dirty, sneaky attack. The notion that only pure, honest, sincere people can be right is a fallacy. The idea that dishonest, dirty crooks must always be wrong is another one. The attempt to discredit the Clinton health care proposal by publishing evidence of the shady financial dealings called "Whitewater" was a classic example of an Ad Hominem attack. If the persona can be discredited, her ideas go down in flames with her. This works in politics because people, bless them, are stupid. It does not work on term papers. Marx may have been a Eurocentric, sexist, racist, ageist pig, but his ideas stand or fall on their own merit. Melville may have beaten his wife, but what does that have to do with the theological mysteries of *Moby Dick*? Jefferson may have kept slaves and not really believed that "all men are created equal," but his writings on democracy are still worth studying.

None of us are saints. If our ideas can be discredited by a listing of our sins, then no ideas anywhere, anytime have any merit, not even yours. Therefore, the personal attacks come out as a wash after all the mud has been thrown. At that point, we then have to go back and do the hard work of considering ideas on their merits and arguments on their logic and evidence anyway. So we might as well skip the Ad Hominem attacks and get to work.

False Choices

Another sneaky way to try to win an argument is by putting the debate in terms of two radical extremes and forcing a false choice: "Either all Americans must some day see the light and accept Christ as their Savior, or we shall all be forced to yield up our liberties to the brutal tyranny of Godless Communism!" Well, maybe there is a third, or a fourth, or several choices in between those two extremes. Presenting a stark choice between two alternatives makes a neat choice, but most of us realize that other alternatives exist.

Non Sequitur

This is Latin for "it does not follow." Basically, this fallacy, like the Ad Hominem argument, involves the attempt to link two things together that really have little to do with each other. The problem here is that of establishing cause and effect and not settling for mere proximity. Farmers finding their cows dry once blamed the losses on the snakes that they found in their barns. Their reasoning was understandable, but the conclusion was a non sequitur. An attempt to tie the financial crisis of 1836 to the rise of Transcendental romanticism requires more than the mere statement of their mutual occurrence. Roosters may see a connection between their crowing and the fact of the sun's coming up. But most of us college professors are smarter than your average chicken.

Many appeals to emotion can be lumped under this category. Descriptions of atrocities by the Serbs may arouse feelings of outrage and a desire to help the Bosnian Muslims, but in any war atrocities can be found on both sides. Before we assume one side is right and worth defending, we might want to avoid jumping to hasty conclusions. It does not follow that horrific examples of atrocities by the Serbs require our intervention against them. Other factors and possibilities need to be examined.

Blaming The Victim

This one is a hot political potato. In some ways, it nicely illustrates the complexity of trying to untangle cause and effect and to establish responsibility in our increasingly relativistic environment.

The date rape issue provides a good example of the problem. Is a woman who goes to a party with a fraternity boy, gets drunk, and then willingingly goes up to his room responsible for the rape that follows? To concentrate on the mistakes of the victim rather than on the crime of the perpetrator is known as "blaming the victim."

While it is true that anyone with any brains ought to know better than to go to fraternity parties in the first place, that does not justify the crime. To concentrate on the mistakes of the bimbo allows the true criminal to get away with rape. Yet where does responsibility lie? Can't the frat boy say with some justification that the girl led him on, that she responded positively every step of the way except for the final one? Indeed, a clever lawyer might well point out that the frat boy is also a victim. Since when is it OK to make derogatory assumptions about males who happen to belong to fraternities?

This argument often goes back to the social constructions of gender roles in America. Women are expected to behave in certain ways in childhood and thus are conditioned to react as they do. Are females really unable to do math, or has society conditioned them to think that they are bad at numbers? If a girl flunks a calculus class, is that her fault or society's? To say it is her fault is blaming the victim.

In that case, then, aren't men also conditioned by their sexist environment to respond as they do? If the girl is not at fault because of her conditioning, then the guy also has to be considered a victim of his conditioning. Where does that leave us? Everyone is a victim and no one is responsible. Many people talk as if they believed that all we have to do is show how a certain anti-social behavior is the result of conditioning and somehow that behavior is excused. But all behavior is the result of conditioning. Thus, the battlefield is littered with effects but there are no causes between here and the horizon. Humanity continues to wallow in its sins but no one at all can be blamed. It's all Adam and Eve's fault, or Eve's, or the snake's. But who put the snake up to it?

The solution is to look at both sides, to realize that both cause and effect exist and to take both into account. A ghetto teenager who mugs a little old lady for her social security check is both a victim of society and a perpetrator of a crime. To look only at the cause of the behavior in social conditioning, as liberals tend to do, or to look only at the effects of those causes in the current moral character of the mugger, as conservatives tend to do, is to miss the larger complexity of cause and effect working together to produce behavior to which we attach either praise or blame. If you can sort this mess out, you should certainly have no problem acing your term paper.

CHAPTER 6
Starting To Write

Do You Need An Outline?

Once you have your voice, your topic, and your argument, you can begin to write. An outline is helpful but it does not have to be explicit. At its most basic, the paper needs only

— a title
— a topic paragraph with a topic sentence that proclaims the argument,
— an explanation of the argument,
— some evidence from the text or texts for the explanation of the argument,
— a counter-argument that you swiftly demolish,
— perhaps some sense of the larger significance of your theme,
— and then a conclusion reasserting the truth of the argument you proclaimed in your opening paragraph.

Outside material such as scholarly articles, book reviews, other books on the same topic certainly add to the quality of the argument and should be included if possible. But you might survive without them. This is your most basic outline.

Since I tend to think in pictures, I like to have an idea of what my argument is going to look like. If I am comparing two points of view, or two texts, or two personalities, I might imagine a zigzag line going back and forth between them: "On this first point, Marx says this..., but Adam Smith says something else. On the second issue, here's Karl again..., but along comes Adam with his rejoinder" and so on. This point-counterpoint approach makes for a basic and easy-to-follow outline.

Another picture of the argument might be that of two legions of lawyers in court, each with its evidence and arguments. After an explanatory introduction, we have two to three pages of Catherine MacKinnon's wonderfully strident rhetoric on the date rape issue; then we have three to four pages of Camille Paglia's colorful prose. After these two blocks, each side gets a chance to refute the other. Then comes another block with our analysis of each or of both together, with appropriate quotations. Finally, we sum it all up for the jurors, treating them respectfully but making sure they understand the points.

If the lawyer metaphor offends you, think of your paper as an army marching to war. You need to have a basic organization, a single purpose, and a unified command. But keep it simple and under control.

The Title

I highly recommend that the writer quickly adopt a working title. The title can always change later, but to have a title at the start is to have a guide, a sense of direction. Whenever I get a paper titled "Paper number 2," I know that the paper is going to be a dud, that the writer does not have anything to say. "Hamlet: An Analysis Of The Play" is not much better. On the other hand, "Emily Dickinson and Allen Ginsberg: Black Holes of the Mind" makes me want to read the paper and see what the writer has to say. This is interesting. Like the headlines on the tabloids at the supermarket checkouts, the titles of your papers need to lure the reader inside. I used to say that they need to be sexy, that like a Victorian woman who lifted her skirt to show a little bit of ankle, they need to titillate the reader and make him or her want to see more of what's under the cover. But I have been accused of "sexual harassment" for even suggesting in class that men might be physically attracted to women and vice versa. That is not politically correct, so I will not say it here.

The Topic Paragraph

Your finished paper must begin with a topic sentence in a topic paragraph. On this I insist. Do not slowly build up to the point you are trying to make. I have no patience for long uphill climbs to the peak. I want to be able to look over the entire view right at the start to get an idea of where I am and where I am going. After you have stated your thesis or argument as boldly as you dare, then in the second paragraph you can go back and fill in the biographical details or whatever else is absolutely necessary. But a paper that begins with the birth of the person being studied is not starting with a topic sentence unless the fact of the person's birth is indeed the subject of the paper.

Often in composition classes (I tend to be more lenient in literature classes), I will cross out the first one or two paragraphs entirely and tell the student to begin with the second or third paragraph and never look back. It often takes students that long or longer to get to their points. Be sure that all of the topic paragraph flows naturally from the topic sentence. Do not try to sneak in some of your supporting details or arguments; these should be reserved for later paragraphs. That is what the rest of the paper is for. A one-word hint or a lively verb that indicates the direction you are taking is great, but keep it short. Remember that your topic paragraph (indeed every paragraph) must have only one topic which is stated in the topic sentence. Remember also that the topic must be an argument. Come out fighting!

Keep The Flow Going

Within the paper it is important to keep the argument flowing smoothly. Remember, your absent-minded physics professor might well get lost. Do not turn your back on her, or as you ascend you will find that she has been left far behind contemplating some bush by the side of the path. Hold her hand by gently reminding her where you are and where you are heading. Do this by repeating key words or phrases that will keep both her and you on track. Knowing how to do this without overdoing it or neglecting it is part of the art of good writing. If, in a paper on racism, you are forced to spend several paragraphs outlining Marx's theory of surplus capital or Freud's analysis of infantile repression, be sure to remind your reader occasionally why this side trip is necessary so she will not think you have simply lost your way. Reassure your poor befuddled reader that you still have the map you started with in mind.

Be sure to use transitions between paragraphs. It may be perfectly clear to you why you are now suddenly talking about what may seem to be a different subject. But it may not be at all clear to your reader. If your next paragraph is offering additional supporting material, write "Furthermore" or some other phrase which suggests this. If you are offering an opposing bit of evidence, write "But" or "Nevertheless" or some other clue to help your reader know what you are up to. It is often a good idea to include a key word from the previous paragraph at the beginning of your new paragraph. Such transition words are important bridges and make the passage between paragraphs much smoother. Do not expect your readers to have the patience to wait and see how it all eventually comes together. We have all watched too much television and expect instant gratification. Do not keep us readers too long in suspense or you are in danger of losing us.

Be Specific

Some teachers like students to begin with general statements and end up with specific examples. Some like papers that begin with the specifics and let the generalities flow from them. No teachers like papers that are all generalities, and only teachers of poetry really like papers that rely on specific images without any explanatory generalizations. Personally, I prefer papers that begin with specifics, that contain many specifics, but that do have occasional generalities when needed to make it perfectly clear to the reader what the point is. As I stated before, it's never safe in a college paper to let the reader infer the point; we professors read too many papers that have no point. We are always suspicious of papers that seem to be implying something but can never quite spit it out. Leave the artsy stuff for your first published novel, or for graduate school at the very least.

By specifics, I mean facts, dates, quotations, information, stories. I want to see pictures in my mind as I read. I cannot comprehend pure abstraction. Idolatrous as it may be, I would clothe even the deity in some sort of form in order for my feeble mind to have something to imagine. If *Newsweek* runs an article comparing education in Russia and the United States, it will not begin with a generality like "Education in Russia is dogmatic and regimented while education in the U.S.A. is permissive and value-free." Instead, it will begin with a word-picture that the reader can see, specific images that bring the comparison to life, like: "In his fourth grade class in Moscow, ten-year-old Gorby Snititovitch sits down quickly after carefully reciting his multiplication tables and the ten most important obligations of a good citizen to the state and its leaders. Meanwhile, in Fairfax, Virginia, ten-year-old Stephen Whitebread draws pictures of airplanes in the margins of his math book while his teacher beams with pleasure at such examples of spontaneous creativity."

Like a political cartoon, the picture says it all. But to be safe, *Newsweek* will then go on to state the generality illustrated by the comparison of the two images. The article will include facts from the two schools, number of hours spent at different specific tasks, the level of instruction reached in a school year, number of pages of literature read and discussed, and so on. There will also be quotations, lively word-pictures themselves that add color and veracity to the points being made. Even the generalities drawn from the specifics will not be allowed to stand without some more specific backing. Education experts or cultural anthropologists will be cited to back up the truth of the comparison and the significance that can be drawn from it.

Specifics give a paper more authority. A student who writes that he can say anything he wants because it is a free country is less convincing than one who writes that he can say anything he wants because freedom of speech is guaranteed by the Constitution of the United States. But the student who writes that she can say what she wants because the First Amendment to the Constitution guarantees that the government can make no law "abridging the freedom of speech" of the people will be the one who everyone listens to with respect. She sounds like she knows what she is talking about. Why? Because she was the most specific.

Being specific applies to whatever kind of paper you are writing. In a history paper, give the most detailed facts possible. Be sure to cite where you found them. Don't tell us what King George said if in fact you can quote a phrase or a line from the old tyrant himself. If you are analyzing Martin Luther King, quote the specific words that prove whatever point you are making. Do not talk in generalities about his "noble Southern rhetoric" or his "Baptist style" without also showing me examples. Do not refer to E.E. Cummings' "peculiar punctuation" without providing evidence. For all you know, I may find his punctuation perfectly normal and may therefore be sitting here wondering what you are talking about.

Sentences

As long as we are beginning to write, let us consider the basic tools of our trade. The sentence is the hammer we use to drive our points home. Each blow must hit a nail. Each sentence must communicate a thought clearly from your mind to that of your reader. Disorganized jumbles of words and phrases cannot do this. Only when the words are arranged in a logical order with a subject and a verb is there a complete thought expressed. The presence of both a subject and a verb is what defines a sentence. Be sure that every sentence has each. Be sure they agree. Sentences can be long or short, complex or simple, but each must contain a clear sense of an actor and some action. Start each sentence with an upper case letter; end each sentence with a period, question mark, or exclamation point. This is basic. Get it right.

Sentences should be varied. Writing the entire paper in short, choppy sentences will make you sound like Mr. Rogers reading *Dick and Jane*. But long, elaborate sentences full of subordinate clauses and other complexities one after another will wear down your reader and produce an impenetrable thicket of words instead of clear, concise prose. There is no happy middle ground here. Mediocre is boring; even God spits the lukewarm out of his mouth. Go back and forth between both.

Paragraphs

A paragraph is the next unit of organization. It needs to be disciplined and unified. All of the sentences within any one paragraph need to be moving in the same direction at the same time. That is, each paragraph needs to be organized around its own topic and must begin with its own topic sentence, a sentence that in one way or another introduces the particular topic that distinguishes that paragraph. The remainder of each paragraph must flow naturally from the topic sentence that heads it. If you find that there seem to be three different ideas in your paragraph, there are two ways to correct the problem. The first is to divide the paragraph into three separate paragraphs. If you do not have enough to say to support an entire paragraph for each of these three points, an alternative is to go back to the beginning of the paragraph and create a new enlarging topic sentence that says something like "Three basic arguments can be presented for the belief that Madonna is in fact the reincarnation of Mary, the mother of Jesus Christ." Your three separate points are now subsets of the topic sentence at the beginning of the paragraph. If you can't imagine a topic sentence that would cover all that is in your paragraph, you'd better break up the paragraph.

CHAPTER 7
Choosing Words

Piss And Urine

What is the difference between "piss" and "urine?"

Technically, they are two different words for the same substance. But we all know which is proper and which improper, which to use in polite company or in formal college papers and which to use in the locker room. Why? Does the fact that doctors prefer "urine" make it acceptable? If so, what caused the doctors or whomever to choose the two-syllable word-sound over the one-syllable word-sound? How do such word choices get made?

The answer is "history."

When William the Conqueror invaded England in 1066, he brought with him a French-speaking aristocracy, imposed on the local Anglo-Saxon population a French ruling class, and created in the process a two-tier social order in which the rulers spoke a Latinate or Romanesque language and the vulgar peasants spoke their native Anglo-Saxon tongue. Hence, the use of Latin came to signify a member of the aristocracy and the use of four-letter Anglo-Saxon words came to signify a peasant. In Mark Twain's *A Connecticut Yankee in King Arthur's Court*, Morgan le Fay has a musician executed because he praised her beautiful "red" hair. For persons of a certain social rank, explained Twain, the word for that color is "auburn." By calling her hair "red," the unfortunate musician was implying that Morgan le Fay was an Anglo-Saxon peasant. By putting this distinction in Arthurian England, centuries before the Norman invasion, Twain was committing an horrendous historical anachronism. Nevertheless, the point is a good one for our purposes.

Our language still carries that same political distinction. Four-letter Anglo-Saxon words like "piss" are, literally, vulgar; Latinate words like "urine" are acceptable if not polite. Ezra Pound, the wacko Fascist poet who taught Hemingway how to write, hated the way English toadied to the Latin oppressor. He raged whenever an American writer used a word like "autumn" seeing that a perfectly acceptable Anglo-Saxon "fall" was available.

In England today, in response in part to the French obsession with criminalizing the use of English words like "le week-end," a group called

"The Pure English Movement" is trying to eliminate Latinate words from English. These folks want to return to pure Anglo-Saxon words. No "copulation" or "fornication" for them!

The larger point is that our word choices, however unconscious, are loaded with political, social, historical, aesthetic, and moral values that we soak up from our cultural history. Very few words are neutral; almost every syllable we utter has the potential to offend some sensitive soul somewhere. It is our responsibility as writers to be aware of the significance of the words we choose, to ask who we might be offending and why, or why not? Why use this word instead of some other? Why this image or metaphor when a newer one might better make our point?

Think about the words you choose. Avoid wasting words. Intransitive verbs, verbs to be and other verbs that simply sit there doing nothing, can almost always be replaced by good, strong, value-loaded action words. Don't say, "The Normans went to England in 1066." Say, the Normans invaded, or sailed, or conquered, or raped, or liberated or some other word that adds more information, color, feeling, or opinion to the story. Eliminate every "there is" and "it is" from your paper. Replace the pronoun with a noun and the intransitive verb to be with an action verb, and be specific. Instead of writing "There was a demonstration on campus yesterday," write "A mob of angry vegetarians destroyed the dean's flower garden in a demonstration against the serving of cooked animal flesh in the campus cafeteria yesterday." Don't choose the first verb or noun that pops into your head. Search around for a better one. That is what makes the difference between good and mediocre writers.

Snobs And Slobs

What we have, and have always had, in American English is a classic battle between conservatives on one side who are afraid that the structures that provide our security are in danger of collapse and radicals on the other who seem willing to embrace any new fad that promises utopia. The conservatives want to retain the rules of grammar and diction and punctuation as handed down to them by their grandfathers. If it was good enough for Jesus, then it's good enough for them. Any change appears to them like the Hun at the gate about to destroy the city. These language snobs can be found in the letters-to-the-editor pages of all our major newspapers bewailing the fate of the republic if people don't follow every jot and tittle of the classical rules.

The position of the radicals, on the other hand, can be illustrated by the argument of a book which came out in the seventies called *The Way it Spozed to Be*. The argument here was that the rules of language reflect the reality of human speech and that we ought not try to standardize the speech patterns of

minority communities but instead allow minority languages an equal legitimacy with so-called "Standard" English. Such language slobs would have us
simply go with the flow carried along on the flood of popular culture wher-
ever that may lead, into whatever Balkanized anarchy.

In fact, we Americans already are a nation of happy slobs and proud of it.
Other nations, like the French, have official bodies which guard the purity of
the national language and pass laws governing what can be said and written in
public. In the United States, we cross our fingers and trust freedom. But as
with so many other aspects of our culture, such as the arguments over gun
control, abortion, and the legalization of pot, there are those who want
stricter control and those who cling to the freedoms of the Bill of Rights.
Traditionally, English professors are expected to be more snob than slob, but
lately the politics of academia have been on the side of minority voices.
Grammar, we are told, is a plot to privilege the distinctive language style of
white male WASPs and thus perpetuate the political dominance of that
cultural class. Hence the teaching of grammar on my campus is considered
politically incorrect. I do it, but I close the doors and whisper.

Even this book, then, is a political act, and the words I choose mark me.
You thus need to think carefully before you choose your words. You need to
be aware of the language battle that is raging around you. Only then can you
choose consciously, and with full knowledge of the consequences, how much
of a snob or how much of a slob you want to be.

Empowering Or Cowering?

Along with this debate goes the perennial pedagogical punchout between
those snobs who insist that students master the traditional rules of grammar
and those slobs who think it more important to empower students by allowing
their oppressed voices to burst out of the shackles of patriarchal, hegemonic
rules. The snobs argue that learning how to write correctly is a tool that
actually empowers students, that students who master the "correct" way to
write can get good jobs, seize control of their lives, and escape from whatever
ethnic ghettos entrap them.

The slobs respond that "correct" means "by the standards established by
white males in order to make everyone else play by the rules of which they are
already the masters." They argue that it is more important that students be
allowed to express themselves in their own idioms and styles and punctuation
and not be made to feel illiterate and stupid simply because they are different.
This, they say, truly empowers them by allowing them the freedom of their
own subcultures.

My own view is that both standard grammar and the liberation of

individual voices are needed. Just as a good jazz musician must first master the
scales and fingering of his of her instrument, so the writer must, as the snobs
insist, master the technicalities of grammar. But just as technical mastery
alone cannot a jazz master make, so a writer must also learn how to dig down
and release his or her own individual soul before the music can swing.
Expression without form is the wailing of an infant, but form without all that
primal energy is as dead as the letter without the spirit.

Cliches

Avoid these like the plague.

Now, when was the last time you personally had to avoid bubonic plague?
Not recently, I'll bet. This is a good example of a cliche, a phrase with no
immediacy, no life, merely a collection of words left over from some other
time repeated to the point where it is used without anyone paying any
attention to what the words say. We get the idea; that's about it.

Emerson had the best lines on this problem. Language, he said, is fossil
poetry. In its youth, it is fresh and alive and creates vibrant pictures. But in
time phrases become fossilized, as dead as rock. It is the writer's job, indeed
the prophet's job, to reconnect words to living things, to create new images
that come alive in the mind and ear. Corrupt men with dead souls simply
repeat stale phrases, "but wise men," says Emerson, "pierce this rotten diction
and fasten words again to visible things; so that picturesque language is at
once a commanding certificate that he who employs it is a man in alliance
with truth and God."

All language is metaphor, and it is up to us to keep the mind alive by
keeping the language alive. We should always be looking for new ways to say
old truths. The first person who said, "It ain't over 'till the fat lady sings" was
a poet. That picture was so true and so to the point that the phrase was
repeated many times over. Within a year it was already a cliche. On election
day, 1992, a group of large ladies got together at the White House gates to
serenade George Bush, momentarily bringing the cliche back to life and
attesting to the power of a common language of shared imagery.

Some phrases, after generations of use, go beyond cliche, no longer even
being pictures, and become ordinary words with no vestige left that they were
once metaphors at all. The word "nitpicking" is my favorite example. We all
know what it means; it means to go at some task in tiny and painstaking detail.
"Nitpicking" is itself a word for a general concept. But what is the picture that
the phrase depicts? What is a nit and why is it being picked? A nit is the egg
case of a crab louse. In the bad old days before the availability of such products as Kwell, mothers in America had to sit down with their children and

examine their heads for lice. After killing as many lice as they could find, they faced the task of sliding the sticky nits off the child's hair one at a time, strand by strand, or of pulling out the individual hairs that had these tiny nits stuck to them. It was a tedious job, and our nineteenth-century ancestors had a vivid picture in their minds when they heard the phrase "nitpicking." Today, it is merely another word. Where is the poet who will create a new word or phrase that depicts this idea with an image true to our modern experience? Perhaps some computer nerd will come up with the perfect phrase for a job that involves millions of tiny chores and painstaking attention to detail.

Emerson and I and English teachers everywhere await that day. We look hard for the student who has a fresh ear for words in new combinations. In the meantime, we point out cliches whenever we recognize them, hoping against hope that some student someday will get the idea and produce the brilliant poetry that will, inevitably, become the cliches of the future.

This is what poets try to do. Some fail, but the successful ones create fresh images that stick in the mind. Camille Paglia, the wild woman of academia, has a way of using language like Joan of Arc swinging a bloody sword. After explaining her theory that Apollonian males, in flight from nature, live in their own created cultural constructs while women, tied by their bodies to nature, are more secure but have less reason to be culturally creative, she creates a picture that captures this notion. Stated in the abstract, this is provocative enough, but the impact of this abstract language cannot compare to the shock of the image she uses to illustrate her point: "Male urination really is a kind of accomplishment, an arc of transcendence. A woman merely waters the ground she stands on." Whatever one makes of her theories, no one can deny that Ms. Paglia is a good writer. She keeps her readers alert.

Ezra Pound told his students to learn new languages to liberate themselves from the idioms and cliches of English. Try Arabic or Gaelic, he told Archibald MacLeish, when MacLeish confessed his inability to escape from cliches. In a letter to his friend Ernest Hemingway, MacLeish complained that Pound "was as full of shit as a cesspool. What's wrong with cliches anyway? Why should we let ourselves be chased up into the ravines just because the good soil had already been farmed before us?"

It was a fair question. And MacLeish had a point. Since all language is "fossil poetry," almost every phrase is a cliche. We cannot write every phrase entirely new or we'll end up as incomprehensible as Gertrude Stein. But that is no excuse for wallowing in the worst of the cesspool. We can strain against fate and fight against habit and, who knows?, maybe even create some new phrases in the process. To leave a new phrase or word behind is to have expanded the collective consciousness and to have more than justified one's existence. Good writers are the heroes who free us from the tyrannies of old cliches of thought and open up the future.

Today, we are witnessing the evolution of another fresh expression through cliche into ordinary language in what may be record time. Once it took generations for phrases to become cliches; today thanks to television and the rest of the mass media, a good phrase can be destroyed in a nanosecond. The "information highway" was the phrase that emerged to describe the Internet, E-mail, and all their associated peripherals. Some thought that the town dump was a better metaphor. After all, one goes into the Internet searching through piles of garbage for the few bits of treasure, and yet as an older saying had it, one man's trash is another's treasure. The "information highway" quickly became such an overused phrase that it developed the stale smell of a cliche. Today, the phrase is already beyond the cliche stage and so standard a word that most writers no longer cringe when they hear it but accept it as another word no different than "nitpicking." Apparently, as space expands, time speeds up, and down we hurtle ever faster through the cosmos.

Say What You Mean – Mean What You Say

Pay attention to what you are actually saying. Pay attention to what your words mean, not just what you intend them to mean. Students come to me constantly with their graded papers in hand whining, "Well, what I meant to say was..." or "But you know what I meant to say..." Sorry, it is your job to mean what you say and to say what you mean, and it is my job to play the innocent, unsuspecting reader. I must respond to what I read on the page, not to give you the benefit of the doubt, and not to read into your confused words what I want you to mean. Don't say "Literally climbing the walls...." unless you are writing about Spiderman. If you mean figuratively, say so. The bottom line in almost all of this is don't pop off with the first thing that comes into your head but think about your words before you write them.

A close relative of the cliche, the mixed metaphor is another example of how we use phrases without paying any attention to the actual picture conjured up by the words. The classic Western Civ 101 mixed metaphor has Dante "standing with one foot in the medieval world while with the other he saluted the rising dawn of the Renaissance."

A published article I use in my composition class refers to women's "underground struggle" for equality. The phrase has a compelling nobility, and I suspect the author used it because it "felt right." But had she thought about it after feeling it, she might have asked whether in fact the women's rights movement in America was ever actually an "underground" movement. The Seneca Falls convention of 1848 was certainly above ground and covered in the press of that day. When the suffragettes marched up Pennsylvania

Avenue and chained themselves to the White House fence in the 'teens, they were hardly hiding underground. If anything, the women's rights movement has been marked by its open and public character right from the start. This is a good example of the use of a word for its vague emotional appeal and not because of its literal meaning. Poets might get away with this sort of sloppiness, but writers of prose should know better.

We are faced here with that vague no-person's land between the realm of emotion and the realm of rational thought. I would be the last person to deny that our rational thoughts are tied to their emotional sources or that writing ought to exist in some mythical rational realm above emotion. The notion that these are two entirely separate phenomena and that thought can occur without emotional entanglement is positivist nonsense. Nevertheless, people say and write "feel" far too often when in fact they mean "think." If your girlfriend comes in wearing a stunning blue dress, you would not say, "I feel that dress is blue." You might, however, say, "I feel stunned by the beauty of that blue dress." As closely tied to each other as they are, good reasons remain for retaining the distinction between feeling and thinking. I am braced for the day some student in math class says, "I feel that one and one is two."

Years ago, in a justifiably famous essay titled "Politics and the English Language," George Orwell pointed out that the way politicians use language tends to confuse the public and destroy the clear communication that is the basis of a true democratic politics. His novel *1984* shows how a totalitarian state can destroy people's understanding of the meaning of words in order to keep those people in a state of oppression. The cure for this is for all of us to use words clearly, to insist that academics and politicians speak to us in a language we all can understand. From the days of the Puritans, the plain style has been at the root of social revolution. While there certainly are those who are language snobs because they want to retain conservative structures of power, there are better reasons on the other side to want to keep the language clear and pure.

Another pet peeve of mine is the current popularity of the word "sensitivity." We must be sensitive to minority concerns, to women's concerns, to the problems of disadvantaged persons of all types. And yet what does the word "sensitive" mean? Does the racist bigot who uses subtly coded phrases to belittle the African-Americans in her class lack sensitivity? If she were not sensitive to the pain her words caused, how could she know exactly where to stick in the pins? One can be both sensitive and racist. On the other hand, if a racist student is causing tension in the class, shouldn't the teacher confront that student in a way that must necessarily offend her? Doesn't it take a fair degree of insensitivity to confront that student and make her shut up? Or should a sensitive teacher understand the depths of pain out of which that racism comes and avoid hurting the poor girl's feelings? What the people who use this term seem to mean is not emotional sensitivity but political adherence. They carefully pick and choose those whom they want to be sensitive to and those whom they want to offend. This seems somewhat dishonest, as if they could push their politics not on the basis of political or ideological merit but on the basis of feeling. It is a leftwing equivalent of the conservative attempt to inflate particular political stands to the stature of patriotism or Godliness and thereby avoid having to debate the issue. Let us puncture all such phony language.

Eugene Genovese, the eminent historian, has argued that when he was in college, the classroom was an ideological war zone in which professors acted as if they were paid "to assault their students' sensibilities, to offend their most cherished values." In that way, students learned to defend themselves with argument, analysis, and evidence. This style of learning is perhaps too narrowly ethnic coming as it does out of a Jewish tradition of argument and confrontation as a way of getting to the truth. But Genovese continues to use it to advantage and argues, "I know no other way to show students, black or white, male or female, the respect that ought to be shown in a place of ideological and intellectual contention." I applaud and submit to you then Genovese's first law of college teaching:

> *Any professor who, subject to the restraint of common sense and common decency, does not seize every opportunity to offend the sensibilities of his students is insulting and cheating them, and is no college professor at all.*

Sexist Language

Should student writers today stick to the traditional use of "he" and "man" to refer to people in general, or should students go along with the current crusade to eliminate gendered language? Well, if that writer wants to pass his course, given the political climate in academia today, he'd better knuckle under fast. Only the fuddiest duddies still defend masculine pronouns as being somehow universal. The rest of us recognize the not-so-subtle implications of using the merely masculine pronoun to mean "people."

The feminist crusade to reshape the language stems from the fact, already noted, that seemingly innocent word choices are loaded with political and social implications. A politically neutral language, if one could imagine such a thing, would be as worthless as a politically neutral politician. We want our words to be taking risks and saying something. What we want is not a value-free language but a language of balanced interest groups. For years the baby doctor Benjamin Spock referred to the baby as "he" and "him." In his last edition of *Baby and Child Care* he tried to make up for a lifetime of error by referring to the baby as "she." In the seventies, a brief movement arose to create the gender-neutral "shem" to replace "him" when that pronoun is used to mean "people." A move was also begun to replace Mrs. and Miss with Ms. Despite the long refusal of the *New York Times* to go along, Ms. has become a normal part of the language; shem never got off the ground.

In this book, you will undoubtedly notice that I use a bit of every alternative. At times I use "him" and assume the masculine; at other times I use "her" and assume the feminine. Occasionally I use the clumsy "his and her" and include both. Since writing ought to reflect real speech, "his/her" or "he/she" are unacceptable. Nobody says "his/her," so nobody ought to write it. In Divinity School, where the gender war was waged with an unholy fierceness, I once solved the difficult problem of which pronoun to use in reference to the deity by writing "s/he/it." The professor was not amused.

The best solution to the gender dilemma is to leap into the plural. There English provides us with the grammatically acceptable and gender neutral "them" and "they." Thus, "Every student must bring his (or his and her, or his/her) books" can become "All students must bring their books." Rewriting your sentence so that the plural pronoun can be used may save you from the wrath of the grader.

Politically Correct Language

"Crippled" is out, except perhaps when referring to airplanes or the Clinton presidency. Why? Because the word has taken on too much offensive baggage over the years. The word conjures up too many images of sick, diseased, and hopeless human wastes. To call someone crippled is to imply that he or she is somehow inferior. In fact, disabled, handicapped, or crippled people really are less able physically, although not mentally or morally. But to admit this is not very nice and allows further unfair insinuations to creep in. So the pressure is on to adopt a value-neutral term, one with no implication of inferiority or inability, a phrase like "differently abled." To use one of the potentially pejorative words is to commit the sin of (I kid you not) "ableism," which is the assumption that able-bodied people are in some ways superior even if that is in fact, in some way, true.

Nor does one avoid this dilemma by avoiding words with negative connotations and using only positive words. After all, one cannot have a positive without a negative. So the use of words with positive connotations, by suggesting that some are better, allows that some must also be inferior. In the academic jargon of the day, even positive language sets up a hierarchy which "privileges" one group over another.

The hope of the PC crowd is that since language influences attitude, a change in language will create changed attitudes. Forty years of "socialist brotherhood" did little for the Serbs and Bosnians who slaughtered each other from opposite sides of the "Bridge of Unity." But hope springs eternal in the American breast. We wish to create utopia even if it means forcing goodness down everybody's sinful throat! Aside from its false assumptions and historical failures, another problem with the plan to change human nature by changing the language is the very real possibility that the old negative connotations will catch up with the new words. It may well be that human emotions control language as much as language controls human emotions. There was a cartoon some years back in *The New Yorker* showing graffiti on a hospital wall that read, "Johnny has mental health." A rose by any other name can still draw blood.

Emerson may have said, "Truth is handsomer than the affectation of love," but he was a romantic essentialist. He actually believed that there was some absolute truth that can be found within the constructed world. But in our confused, relativistic world where there is no knowable truth, affectation is all we really have. So like a Victorian lady, we smile and lie hoping that somehow the world of words we thus create can replace this dung heap we inherited. Politically correct language is an attempt to deny what once was naively called truth in order to create instead a brave new world, a verbal utopia, in which accidental, or natural, or socially constructed differences no longer exist. Language, after all, is a virtual reality helmet. If you don't like this world, unstrap it and try on another.

Not that I have anything against niceness, mind you. But when the two values clash, I prefer the truth, however mean and ugly. Being something of an old-fashioned essentialist myself, if not a downright Puritan, I am naive enough to believe that outside of the virtual reality language helmets we all wear, something exists. That something, whatever it is, call it reality or truth, is not the artificial socially-constructed self but the SELF, the context out of which we arose and within which we live and move and have our being. Our perceptions of that reality may be distorted and blocked by the virtual reality language helmets of our socially constructed selves. Deus may be absconditus. But S/He/It is still out there somewhere, still handsomer than the affectation of love.

Politically correct language, by substituting niceness for truth, would abandon any attempt to break out of these virtual word cages. It would accept the cages of our social constructions as inevitable and turn to the effort to beautify the cages. But some of us are not willing to accept even utopian cultural cages. We would prefer to continue to struggle to take the helmets off, to break out of the cages. We would continue the western tradition of leaving Egypt and risking the dangers of the wilderness in the hope of arriving some day in some promised land. We would rather light out for the territory than be civilized. Bitter though it is, people in wheelchairs unable to use their legs are still cripples.

Good writers try to tell what is at least to them the truth and to communicate their human value judgements. Writing stripped of all value judgement or opinion is as boring and dry as a legal brief. We may be conditioned and all our values may be virtual and not actual realities, but even then we believe what we believe because we believe it. We can only get outside of the virtual reality helmets by trying to find the cracks in the reality presented, by chasing down what seems to be real until it reveals itself as virtual or actual. We can only get to whatever ultimate truth may exist by going through the relative beliefs that appear to us as truths. We need to confess the stupidities we really believe and not pretend to believe in somebody else's constructs.

Money is a good example of this. The dollar bills in our wallets are socially constructed fictions. They only seem to have value, but they are in fact pieces of paper with writing on them. Their value is only apparent, not real. That value is not in the paper but in the faith we have in the paper. But even those who insist that our perceptions of reality and our sense of value are socially constructed will not open their wallets and hand out the bills therein.

So do try to resist the politically correct pleas for niceness. Tell it straight. Tell your truth however awkward, embarrassing, or painful. Sin boldly.

The Literary And Historical Present

Write about texts in the present tense; write about events that occurred in the past in the past tense. The book is alive even if the author is dead. Therefore, in *Moby Dick* Captain Ahab says, "Be the White Whale principle or the White Whale agent, I shall wreck my hate upon him." But Herman Melville wrote those words in 1851. Ahab lives on, but Melville, the author, is history. Note however that Melville's voice in the text like Ahab lives on. If you remember that books are considered to be alive, you should have no problem.

When using different tenses, do be careful. If you are writing in the past tense and you refer back to an event that occurred even earlier, be sure to use the pluperfect "had." When you return to the past time in which you started, be sure to return to the past tense. One way to remain clear and to avoid confusing your readers is to keep each tense consistent within a paragraph and not bounce back and forth between different time zones in any one paragraph. Keeping your tense straight will go a long way toward helping keep your reader straight. Remember where you are and when you are.

CHAPTER 8
"Robert Frost: Gentle New England Satanist"

To give you an idea of how this game can be played, let us dance through one example, not of the finished product, but of the process of writing an analytical essay.

Let's say that you have been given the assignment to write about a poem. Let's make it one that every American schoolkid is familiar with, Robert Frost's "Stopping By Woods on a Snowy Evening." Assuming you have no idea yet what you intend to say, begin your writing with a simple description of the generally obvious literal facts. Make it clear that you understand the literal meaning, that indeed you actually read the words. We professors, cynical bastards that we are, actually look for that. Tell me that "Stopping by Woods" is the picture of a person riding through woods in the winter time and stopping to "watch the woods fill up with snow." Use brief phrases or significant individual words from the text as evidence. At the very least, this proves you read the poem. Imagine a working title, something hopelessly vague like "The Meaning of Frost's Famous Poem." This at least gives you something to begin with.

Once the literal facts have been described — a fairly easy task in this example — then begin your ascent. Step beyond the literal and ask, What else might be going on here? What is suggested? What can we learn that isn't obvious?

A popular English-major approach is to describe the poet's use of one or some of the standard poetic conventions, dissonance, assonance, meter, rhyme scheme, and so on. By itself such explication is merely clever. It reveals the writer's ability to identify these conventions and to handle the jargon. But it says nothing important about the work as literature. If you wish to follow this path, you must not only reveal your ability to identify the types, you must also say how the use of the particular convention influences the meaning of the work, how the structure of the poem reflects or undercuts the meaning, literal and suggested, of the words. This is difficult and subtle; the undergraduate is probably going to be safer sticking with the meaning of the words and not getting too deeply into the subtleties of meter and rhyme. That this poem can be sung to the tune of Hernando's Hideaway is an embarrassment better left to talk-show hosts or Ph.D.s in cultural studies and prosody.

Perhaps a word or phrase of the poem suggests something not clearly spelled out in the literal facts. A popular interpretation imagines that the who of "Whose woods these are" is God, that "his house" in the village is the local church. If you apply this reading to the rest of the poem, it might lead to a moralistic interpretation of "miles to go before I sleep." Life, it seems, is a moral duty; if we faithfully do our moral duty, then we will be rewarded after the end. Perhaps the poet is on a pilgrimage of some sort? If so, then the literal pilgrimage of the poet's journey may stand for some other, more abstract, pilgrimage. Perhaps life itself is this pilgrimage? We must all trudge along and do our duty.

But then still more ascent is possible. What is a pilgrimage? Define the term. What do we know about Robert Frost that would illuminate this idea? How does this apply to our own lives? Is Frost suggesting to us that we all go on pilgrimages? Suddenly, we find ourselves echoing Chaucer's "Canterbury Tales" and the roots of English literature. Is there a connection? What does that tell us about ourselves? Perhaps the most significant thing to be learned from this poem is the way in which by responding sympathetically to this poem we (or some of us) are still caught up in the Christian worldview of our ancestors, that some (too many?) of us are still, to use the Chaucerian metaphor, Englishmen who long "to go on Pilgrimages." Or if we are bored to tears by such Christian moralism, that tells us something too.

Can you then go back to the poem and rereading it with this possibility in mind find any more hints however subtle? Perhaps. The main action of the poem is the poet's stopping. There is at least a tension between his stopping to look at the deep dark woods and the "miles to go." The horse certainly asks if stopping is not "a mistake." The horse of course is an animal, a possible symbol of the natural. If nature and God urge us onward to our moral duty, what then is the force that calls us to stop and contemplate the "dark and deep" woods? Satan?

That's it! Robert Frost was a satanist! At least, he was tempted by satanism, whatever the Hell that is. The evidence is there in the poem. You can bow to the New Critics' demand for strict textual interpretation and the search for a unifying theme by showing how the entire poem sets up a conflict between the call to do our Godly duty and some deeper, darker impulse from the Satanic forests, which themselves may be, as the wilderness often is, a symbol for the wilderness of the soul.

Then, to appease the need to contextualize the poem, if you look at even a brief biography, you might learn that Frost once tried to kill himself in the Great Dismal Swamp, that he was considered by many to be an egomaniac and a tyrant, that he bullied his wife and children, that he pulled a gun once on his wife in front of his daughter, that his son committed suicide. There is plenty of evidence in Frost's life, to say nothing of his many other poems, to support any argument you might like to construct about the specific evils by which he was tempted and to which he succumbed. Rumor has it that he was even a Republican.

Now that you have your interpretation, you can go back and change your working title to a more appropriate title, something like "Robert Frost: Gentle New England Satanist." Now there's an ironic title an English professor cannot resist. Then you can write your new topic paragraph boldly stating the basic theme:

> *Although considered by many to have been a gentle New England poet of nature, Robert Frost was in fact a secret Satanist, and a close reading of such poems as "Stopping By Woods on A Snowy Evening" reveals not the Godly purposefulness seen by some critics but a terrible enslavement to the Devil.*

In the second paragraph, you can make use of your original effort to present your literal understanding of the surface of the poem. You need to prove to the teacher that you read and understood at least the most obvious level of the poem, and you need to make sure that our absent-minded physics professor knows that you know the basic facts, images, and words. Otherwise, he will never buy your interpretation.

Be sure, always, to present objections, if only to demolish them. Imagine the voice of some sentimental sap who still clings to the pious reading of the poem. Show that you understand the objections of the disbelievers, and then show how shallow or misguided they are. Perhaps you should follow up in several more paragraphs by showing that you also have read and understand one or two of these more traditional naive interpretations of the poem. You might want to spend a paragraph or two exploring some of the reasons why those older critics missed the boat. What blinded them to the obvious? Were they part of a conspiracy to bedevil the nation's youth by foisting satanic poetry on them while pretending it had pious purposes? Or was there some way in which their own self-interest was furthered by their interpretation? What was there in the old pious readings that was of benefit to these saps?

Feminists argue that the emphasis in literature classes on white male authors like Frost is part of a subtle effort to perpetuate the lie that only white male Protestants from New England have had anything worthwhile to say. By doing this, perhaps without realizing it, these white male professors trained in the New England tradition are reinforcing their own positions of power and authority within the culture. Perhaps the moral duty Frost was recommending we all stick to, presumably, was the oppressive demand that blacks stay in the fields and women stay in the kitchen? As a white male New England

Protestant myself, I find this line of reasoning utterly ridiculous, but I have to grant that it is a perfectly possible argument to try to make.

Among other perfectly possible, if utterly ridiculous, interpretations, Marxists might talk about Frost's marketing and commodifying his art, to say nothing of his Republican politics. The emphasis on ownership, "his house... his woods... my little horse... But I have...," suggests an obsession with control and possession. Frost, so his biographers tell us, was a careful man with a penny who kept every scrap of paper he doodled on to sell to equally materialistic collectors. Feminists can explore his role as patriarchal tyrant and defender of traditional male hegemonic values. What, after all, do we make of the unrelenting repetition of "his house," "his woods," "his harness bells?" African-Americans might want to explore Frost's use of "darkness" as a signifier for evil. Clearly, the interpretive possibilities are almost limitless. There is even a school of interpretation, certainly beneath my contempt, which argues that what is left out is really what a work is all about, that our silent denials reveal our real selves. If no mention is made of homosexuality or apartheid in South Africa, that could be significant. Just what is Frost trying to hide, anyway, and why is he trying to hide it?

That nonsense aside, one of the main attractions of the poem, like all great literature from the Bible through *Moby Dick* to "Thelma and Louise," is that it is specific enough to be interpreted but vague enough to allow us to project our own concerns onto it. We need to remember not to succumb to either extreme but to retain both text and context. We do not want to return to the New Critics and the tyranny of some deep inner meaning cleverly hidden in the text, but neither do we want to leave the text behind as we chase after our own personal or ideological butterflies.

Once the naive, sentimental reading of the poem has been dealt with, or the cynical, oppressive reading of the poem has been exposed, we can go on and reveal by a close reading just how we arrived at our terrifying revelation. Here, we need to bring in whatever other clues we can find in our reading of the rest of the poem. To whom did Frost make those "promises to keep?" And what might those promises have been? Perhaps Frost sold more than scraps of paper? How great a price might an ambitious man pay for fame and literary power? What now happens to the repetition of the last line, "and miles to go before I sleep?" Instead of a holy pilgrimage, is this perhaps a Satanic mission? And doesn't the lock-step repetition of that last line send a chill through the reader's soul?

In later paragraphs, we can bring in the outside facts from Frost's life, or perhaps some evidence from one or two of his other poems (Just what was that "other road" in the yellow wood less travelled by?). For these, we may have to quote biographers, literary critics, class notes. We may have to use our imaginations. But as long as our reasoning is logical and the evidence valid, who can call us wrong?

Near the end, you need to say something about the "use" of your revelation, that is the significance for us all. You might add an appropriately chilling message. Perhaps we should be less naive. Satan is everywhere. Let us re-examine Donald Duck and Mickey Mouse: capitalists? yes — sexists? certainly. But satanists? That had gotten by us before. Quick, run to the den and turn off the TV before another generation of Americans is corrupted.

Remember these rules: present your arguments, present your evidence, define your terms, explain how your evidence proves your argument, and don't forget to include opposing views which you then demolish. To present only one side of an issue is unconvincing and ends up sounding like propaganda. A paper on abortion that merely states the argument that abortion is murder is not going to convince those people who have heard that argument but are still unconvinced. You need to take their counter-argument into account and show them why they nevertheless should be convinced. This has the additional advantage of making it appear as if you have greater control over the whole of the debate so that even if you are wrong it gives your paper more authority. Quote from some published analysis of the poem to prove that you are not attacking some straw man.

At the end of the paper, conclude with a paragraph that sums up your basic argument Do not try to bring in new evidence or new ideas in the conclusion. If you have more to say, or a new idea, go back and put it into the body of the paper where it belongs. And in your concluding paragraph, refer back to the topic paragraph, to the beginning of the paper with some allusion to the language or the imagery of the opening. This brings your paper full circle and neatly ties it up in a tightly closed bundle. Restate your argument and your conclusion. Drive the stake finally deep into Frost's cold heart and nail down the coffin lid. Read the poem again, and lock the door.

CHAPTER 9
Some Basic Corrections

The symbols used here are my own and are not in universal use, at least not yet. I prefer not to use many of the standard names and phrases because I fear that too many students get lost in memorizing nomenclature and never spend enough time worrying about why these errors are forbidden. To understand the rules that govern grammar is more important than to know one hundred different phrases for various mistakes. Therefore, I have tried to find new ways of identifying common errors so that students will know why I think they are wrong.

ONW – Omit Needless Words

Taken from Strunk and White's famous *Elements of Style,* this simple rule applies more often than any other to papers I correct. I need to get a stamp made with this on it. I follow Ray Kroc's rule, "K.I.S.S.," "Keep it Simple, Stupid." The fewer words in which something can be said the better. Don't use eight words when two will do. Don't say "Following is the next argument in support of the proposition here under consideration;" say "Next,..."

NAS – Not A Sentence

A sentence must have at least a subject and a verb and usually but not always an object. Sometimes phrases will appear that do not have a subject or a verb. Like this one. More often than not, these sentence fragments will be descriptive phrases tacked to the ends of sentences. They should be preceded by a comma and not treated as a separate sentence. Never mind what *Time* does; *Time* is wrong. You can be creative later. But you must learn how to do it right before you can appreciate the liberties involved in doing it wrong.

MM – Misplaced Modifier

A misplaced modifier is what some grammar books call a "dangling modifier" or a "dangling participle." Whether you intend it or not, a descriptive phrase at the beginning of a sentence modifies the very first noun that follows. Hence, if you write, "Walking down the street, a piano fell on my head," you are saying that a piano was walking down the street. I once saw on a paper the sentence, "Being the early sixties, democracy was not yet known in New Jersey." According to this sentence, democracy is "the early sixties."

The sentence is weird enough without that misplaced modifier. I also have in my overflowing file of grammatical horrors an ad for Wendy's which reads, "As our valued guest, we guarantee to serve you" the best. In this sentence, "we" are our own "valued guest." If Wendy's wants to serve itself, it should at least make the word "guest" plural to agree with the plural "we." This is a mistake that readers of *The New Yorker* and other language snobs love to snicker at. If you do not want to look ridiculous, avoid misplaced modifiers.

// – A Problem With Parallelism

Perhaps due to its Germanic origins, English demands order. It loves consistency, symmetry, parallel structure. Things in a series must all be in the same form. Do not say, "I love swimming, jogging, and sex." In this example, "sex" is not the same verb form as "swimming" and "jogging." Say "having sex." Or change the first two verbs: "I love to swim, to jog, and to ..." (you choose your own verb here). If you are using the plural, stay with the plural. If you are in the past, stay there. If you have to change to the present, indicate clearly that you are doing so, perhaps with a whole new paragraph. Remember to be consistent.

This principle can be extended to cover those other errors of number and person that are far far too common. If you begin with the first or second or third person as your subject, stick with it. Never write, "If one looks their best, you will always get laid." If you have a singular subject, use a singular verb. Note that "everyone," "anyone," "no one," "neither," are in fact singular and take singular verbs: "Everyone in this class is [not are] in danger of flunking." The committee is.... but the members of the committee are.... All you need do to get these right is to pay attention to the meaning of the words. Though it does not always seem so, there is some logic to the rules of American English. Curiously, British English makes the collective noun take a plural verb: "The English Team are playing in France this weekend." But they've been going downhill since Cromwell.

Here is exhibited one of the irrational aspects of English usage which you simply have to accept. A Cambodian student of mine, fresh off the boat, had a hard time making plurals. In his native language, "Ten dog" clearly indicated that there was more than one dog. He didn't see the need for the "s" after dog to indicate more than one. "Just do it," I said. He did. When we got to verbs, he put his logical, computer nerd foot down. "Why do you put an s after the verb if the subject is singular?" he cunningly asked. "Why 'he shoots,' but 'they shoot'? Shouldn't the plural subject be indicated with an s and not the singular? Shouldn't it be 'he shoot' and 'they shoots'?" Logically, what he said made sense. Ever reasonable, sensitive, and full of compassion, "Just do it," I said.

AWK – Awkward

We paper-graders use AWK when a sentence is so confusing that we cannot or do not have the time or patience to try to straighten it out. If you cannot tell that something sounds wrong, read the sentence out loud or have someone else read it to you. Most native English speakers will recognize when there is something wrong. It is usually better to start all over again with such sentences than to try to straighten them out. Sometimes if a sentence seems truly hopeless, the best and easiest cure is to put it out of its misery. They shoot horses, don't they?

OOG – One Step Beyond "AWK"

"OOG" is an unpleasant gut reaction to a string of disastrous errors.

BB – Back-To-Back

These are rare. Most college writers have learned to avoid them, but they do appear on occasion. They are the placing of the same words or phrases at the end of one sentence and the beginning of the next. Clearly, when this occurs, there is some way to combine the two sentences smoothly into one. Hence, it is really a subset of "ONW." Example: "I saw the dog. The dog was running away."

Typo – Typographical Error

It isn't necessary for me to say that typos are to be avoided. You know that. But it is necessary for me to stress the importance of proofreading your text before you hand it in. The reason is as much political as grammatical. A paper that you did not bother to proofread even once for obvious mistakes is clearly one that you don't care about. And if you don't care about it, why should I? On the other hand, a typo corrected by pen, however messy, at least shows that you cared enough to look for errors and correct them. If so many such corrections start to make the page look like chaos, then perhaps you should seriously consider typing it over again.

Word-processing introduces its own dangers. For example, even using a spell-check program does not tell you if you spelled "your" as "you." Most programs cannot tell if in erasing some mistake you accidentally left in three words of the original sentence. Do not rely on technology to do your scud-busting for you. You must reread every blessed word yourself carefully. Typos are like rocks in a New England garden. No matter how many you find and remove, the next time you look a big one will be staring you in the face. Nevertheless, keep looking and find as many as you can.

CHAPTER 10
Some Common Stupid Mistakes

We all make them, God knows. I spelled my graduate thesis advisor's name wrong on every sheet of my thesis proposal. Nevertheless, such mistakes are to be avoided if possible. Here are some of the most familiar that I encounter in papers from Freshman Comp to graduate seminar.

Its, It's, and Its'

This one is pretty simple once you have it pointed out to you. It is the exception to the rule in English about how we make possessives and contractions. We usually make the possessive by adding apostrophe (') s. We make a contraction in the same way. Hence "it is" and "of it" should both be "it's." But this way chaos lies. So once upon a time an arbitrary decision was made that "it is" has priority and deserves the honor of the apostrophe. "Of it" must therefore be satisfied to live without one. Just remember:

it is = it's   of it = its

As for "its'," a construction I have indeed seen, try to imagine the sentence that would need a possessive of the plural "its." For the only one I can imagine, the word "it" would have to appear several times on the blackboard in green chalk, and someone would have to be saying something about "the its' color."

The Possessive

As long as we are on the topic of apostrophes, let's deal with the possessive. Everyone knows how to make the possessive, but not everyone knows how to distinguish the plural from the singular. It's very easy. If the thing or things being possessed are being possessed by more than one thing, and the corresponding noun has an "S" at the end, the apostrophe goes outside the "S." A student who writes about "my fathers' face" is saying literally that he or she has more than one father and all those fathers share one face. Since most humans can have only one father, it should be "my father's face" or perhaps if the father is the two-faced type "my father's faces."

Dealing with the plural possessive can get tricky when the singular form of the word ends in "S." If there is only one syllable, simply treat the word as you would any other: "my boss's foot." With two or more syllables, you have problems. And here we reach the horizon of the known world. Beyond this point, truth belongs to the person with the best argument. There is no absolute. For every expert who claims authority for a particular answer, there are two other equally valid authorities with different answers. (I was criticized at my doctoral thesis defense because I had written repeatedly about "Jonathan Edwards' theology." Luckily, I was —oddly for me— prepared with a citation from some obscure grammar book which said that if the emphasis is on the first syllable, the final "S" of the possessive could be omitted. But it was close.)

A more obscure but equally noteworthy mistake is the use of the possessive apostrophe within a possessive. It is hard to resist the temptation to write "That was a mighty wonderful speech of Churchill's." Well, the possessive is already there in the "of." To what does the "'s" refer? There is a noun missing. "of Churchill's maid?" "of Churchill's dog?" We will never know. If you can't say "That was a wonderful speech of Churchill," say "That was a wonderful speech Churchill gave." Sometimes, a writer has to go back and straighten out whole sentences in order to fix a small problem.

The Split Infinitive

Here we separate the true language snobs from the language slobs. It is important to realize that grammar is by and large an arbitrary convention. Moses did not bring it down from Sinai. It changes constantly, especially in America. There is no board of official grammarians in this country that sits and decides the rules. These evolve through usage. What one person sees as a mistake might be seen by another as the cutting edge of change. The important thing is not to learn the rules but to learn the arguments. Second rate minds know all the rules but only the rules; first rate minds know all the rules and all the objections to them. If your English grader has a second rate mind, it is up to you to decide how you are going to react. Either you rigidly follow his rules, or you prepare your first rate mind to point out the problems after he hands you back your D. Understand that we graders cannot tell the difference between a clever innovation consciously contrived and a stupid mistake blundered into, and it is our duty to deny the student the benefit of the doubt. It is the student's duty to communicate his or her knowledge to us.

Nowhere does the arbitrary nature of the grammar wars come out more clearly than in disputes over the split infinitive. You all, I trust, recognize this error. An infinitive is the "to" plus a verb, to go, to swim, to cheat, to steal, etc. The traditional language-snob law demands that no words ever be inserted between the "to" and the verb. To do so is to split the infinitive. Yet infinitives are split all the time. What is the mission of the Starship Enterprise? "To boldly go where no man has gone before," and to boldly split infinitives where no infinitive has been split before. They did change the wording in the new series you will be glad to note. The new mission is "to boldly go where no one has gone before." The only change is a clear indicator of modern sensitivity to sexist language; "man" has been changed to "one" but the split infinitive remains. In the bold new world of the future, split infinitives are OK, but sexism is a sin.

I personally do not care if an infinitive is split as long as the meaning is clear. I force composition students to follow the old law exactly in the hope that in the future when they do split infinitives they will feel a twinge of shame. If they must do it, I want them at least to intentionally split (sic) the infinitive and not do it by accident or from ignorance. In my general literature classes, I allow split infinitives to go unpunished as long as there is not more than one word in the split. Hence, I am neither slob nor snob but wishywashily in the middle. In no case is it OK to accidentally or intentionally split an infinitive with more than one word.

"Hopefully" And Other Controversies

As long as we are in the realm of the language snob, the other taboo besides the split infinitive that causes these folk to foam at the mouth is the misuse of the adverb "hopefully." The problem here is an interesting one. The protectors of the language fear that misuse of words ruins those words for everyone. And they are right. Just as the misuse of any liberty eventually leads to the loss of that liberty for us all, so the misuse of words leads to the destruction of our common literary heritage. Sometimes this does not matter. Sometimes it does. I personally regret the loss of "disinterested" as a word. It used to be a positive word that meant a state of perfect objectivity. Judges were supposed to be disinterested. Today it has come to mean "uninterested." But we already have a term for uninterested. We still need disinterested. But I cannot use it in its original meaning and expect to be understood. Most literate people fight stubbornly to retain the unique meaning of "unique." This word means one and only one. Therefore, you cannot have highly unique, very unique, more unique, or any of the other ways in which people use the word to mean "rare." We already have "rare;" let's keep "unique" unique.

"Hopefully," however, exists in that grey area between the snobs and the slobs. According to the grammar purists, "hopefully" is an adverb defining an action to be used only when an action is done with hope or in a hopeful manner as in such sentences as "Hopefully, he took the exam" or "Hopefully, he bought a lottery ticket." But most slobs, and most of us are slobs, use it in place of "I hope." If I say, "Hopefully, I took the exam," wouldn't you answer, "Don't you know whether you did?" The sentence is ambiguous and can be read either way. William Safire, the author of the "On Language" column for

The New York Times and one of the nation's leading experts on all things pertaining to the American use of words, is willing to let the original use of hopefully as an adverb be replaced by its use as a substitute for "I hope." There is actually little he can do to stop it. The change is here. But in English departments across the country, purists are fighting fiercely like King Canute to stop the oncoming tide. If you do not want to be a statistic in their struggle, you'd better be careful when you use "hopefully."

Adjective Or Adverb?

Most students by the time they are in college know that an adjective describes a noun, a thing, and an adverb describes an action, how something is done, and that most adverbs end in "ly." But the problem arises when the adverb does not end in "ly" and the writer is not sure which word is the adverb and whether in fact an adjective or an adverb is called for. One can only learn the exceptions that cause the most problems. Here are two of the worst.

To "do good" means to do good works. The noun defined by the adjective "good" is understood. To "do well" means to do in a good manner. In idiomatic American speech, it specifically means to be making money. If someone asks, "How are you?" and you answer, "I'm doing good," you are in fact saying that you are involved in doing good works. If you want to say that you are getting along OK, say, "I am doing well." My favorite phrase that helps to distinguish these is the statement often quoted about the Quakers: "They came to America to do good, and they did right well."

Even more troublesome is the "feeling bad" and "feeling badly" dilemma. This is a useful distinction to grab because it vividly illustrates the difference in meaning and hence the importance of knowing what it is you are actually saying. To "feel bad" is to feel sick; to "feel badly" is to have numb or clumsy hands and thus not do the act well. Just remember the phrase, "She felt bad because he felt badly." Or if you find that too sexist, put in the gender pronouns of your own choice.

The sign "Think Smart" is like the bumper sticker "Think Snow." Since "smart" is not an adverb, there is an implied "about" stuck in there. "Think Smartly" is what all of those stupid signs should say.

Prepositions And Their Pronouns

By now you are undoubtedly getting pretty irritated that I still haven't told you what those horrendous sinners did to bring down the wrath of

Stanley Marcus, he of the "personal antipathy" to the misuse of the personal pronoun following a preposition. Well, here it is.

Prepositions always take the objective form of the pronoun. The objective form is the form when the pronoun is an object; the subjective is the way you would use it as a subject. Just think of a simple sentence: "She shot him." She is the subject, the actor; him is the object, that to which the action was done. All prepositions take the objective form. For, with, between, to, by, into, out of, etc., etc., etc. all take an objective pronoun. This is true even when there are two pronouns connected by a conjunction. Hence, the girlfriend should have said, "There is so much love between you and me," not "you and I." You wouldn't say "He shot I" would you? Of course not. The objective form is "me." There are still English teachers in fourth grades across the country who think that it is always better to use "I" than to use "me." They are responsible for ruining that poor girl's life. Don't let them ruin yours.

Fewer And Less

It may surprise you to learn that there is a difference between these two words; "fewer" and "less" aren't interchangeable, although they're so often used incorrectly that it seems as though they might be. If you become confused about which word to use, follow this simple rule: "fewer" is for things you can count, and less is for things you can't such as abstract ideas. Therefore, it would be "fewer elephants" but "less noise," "fewer dollars" but "less money," "fewer bigots" but "less hatred." All those illiterate signs in the Safeway should read, "Express lane, ten items or fewer." Once you master the difference, the ability to make the correct distinction between "less" and "fewer" will immediately set you apart from the pack and help elevate you to the status of grammar guru.

Who And Whom

This is similar to the preposition problem. There really is a sane, logical rule for when to use "who" and when to use "whom." Who is the subjective form; whom is the objective form. Thus, use "who" when the word is the subject; use "whom" when it is the object. "The girl whom he kissed" is good grammar, but so is "the boy who kissed her." The problem comes when the who phrase gets confused with its surrounding sentence. The rule is to take the who phrase out of context and look at the who phrase all by itself to determine if the "who" is doing the acting or being done to. "Good grades are possible for whoever deserves them." In this example, the preposition "for" immediately suggests to the ear that "whom" is needed. Didn't I just say in the section on prepositions that prepositions always take the objective form of the pronoun? Isn't "for" a preposition? And isn't "whom" the objective form?

Yes to all three questions. BUT one must look at the who phrase and only the who phrase. "For whoever deserves them" is correct because in the phrase "whoever deserves them," "whoever" is the subject and "them" is the object. These can be tricky; watch out.

Even nastier is the who phrase that makes the "who" look as if it is the object of the phrase when it isn't. If the sentence read "for whoever I think deserves them," doesn't "I" become the subject and "who" the object, making "whom" correct? No! Why not? Because "I think" is a parenthetical aside, an additional bit of information. "Deserves" is still the verb of the who phrase. Cute, eh?

Unclear Referents

These come in two flavors: pronouns that could refer to any one of a number of nouns, and pronouns that could refer to absolutely anything. "Whenever dogs bite people, they get put to death." To what does the "they" in this sentence refer? Is it the dogs or the people? The referent for "they" is unclear and thus this sentence needs to be fixed. Either the dogs or the people need to be put to death.

The pronoun "it" is too often used without any referent at all. This leaves the job of figuring out what is being talked about to the imagination. And since most people think about sex most of the time, the result is all those bumper stickers saying "Divers do it deeper," "Conservationists make it last longer," "Bakers make it rise," "Teachers do it in front of the class," or whatever your profession is. A furniture company in the Washington, DC area advertises, "You'll love it at Levitz." Well, I love it, but I never considered doing it on one of the beds in the Levitz showroom. Nevertheless, in such advertising the use of the unclear referent "it" is a deliberate attempt to exploit the ambiguous potential of the word. When done deliberately like this, such use of "it" is clever; when done unintentionally, it is just stupid. Note the ambiguous "it" in the last line of the introduction to this book; am I referring to life or to grammar? Here, the ambiguity is intentional.

I, Me, Mine; I, Me, Mine; I, Me, Mine

Ms. Snigglebottom undoubtedly taught you never to use "I" but always to be objective. It is necessary at the high school level to pry students away from the endless contemplation of self and to get them to think about the world outside themselves. Adolescent writing can be painfully narcissistic. Hence, high school teachers forbid the use of "I" in order to control the excesses of adolescence. Once students have made it to college, however, things which were forbidden to them when they were children become real possibilities, even sometimes necessities. We teachers really do want to know what you think. The purpose of your writing a paper on Jonathan Edwards is to show the world what Jonathan Edwards looks like from your unique perspective as a human being. Each one of us is different; some are white, some black, some male, some female, some Asian, some gay, most in fact a unique mixture of some of the above. Your paper is the expression of your unique viewpoint. What you then need is a balance of subjective opinion and objective fact. In high school, you were told to leave the "I" out and merely be objective. Now you need to bring the subjective "I" back into your analysis. You can do this without ever actually using the word "I" if that word becomes too bothersome. After writing, "I believe that George Will is a pompous ass," edit out the "I believe that." We know that the rest of the sentence is your opinion. Your subjective point of view is clearly present. Hence, you get the best of both worlds, subjective color and energy with objective language, logic, and fact. Even George Will would approve.

Spelling

What can I say about spelling except: "Get it right!"

Poor Dan Quayle will forever serve, whatever else he does, as an example of the ridicule that might someday be heaped upon you too if you never do learn how to spell potato.

As one of the worst spellers in Christiandom, I warn my students not to relax therefore but to worry more. For if I recognize a misspelling on their papers, they are really in trouble. Nothing makes you look stupider than not knowing how to spell. Many common mistakes need to be dealt with individually, and the grammar handbooks often list pages of these. Remember, for instance, that there is "a rat" in "separate." You will then be less tempted to spell the word "seperate." Beware also of words that sound right but are slightly off. These can be clever if intentional, but we teachers cannot always tell and we rarely give you the benefit of the doubt. One student of mine spelled hypocrisy "hippocracy." I defined that as government by hippos. Another student wrote of some people "conjugating" in the corner of the room. She meant "congregating," I think. Such malapropisms are often funny. I once received a paper on Malcolm X in which the student said that Malcolm X was angry and eloquent "because of the manor in which he was raised" and that he was discriminated against "for the soul reason of race." The class howled; the student, although unnamed, blushed and slunk under his chair. Don't let it happen to you.

Hyphens

These are probably underused. A hyphen in time can save you a great deal of embarrassment. Note that many of these technical problems are considered errors because they create confusion and ambiguity. They force the reader to stop and go back over the sentence to figure out what is being said. In a string of adjectives before a noun, each word is assumed to define the noun. Is a small dairy farmer a small person or a person who farms a small dairy? If you mean a farmer of small dairies, a hyphen between the two adjectives makes your meaning clear. How about processed baby food? Yum!

Note also that at the end of the line a hyphen should be used to separate a word too long to fit the space. Such forced separations should occur between syllables or between a double consonant. Always hyphenating correctly shows the reader just how intelligent you are.

Must Of Alot Of Attitude

I could of course go on forever, but let me leave this category with a lumpen collection of ugly errors. The verb form "must have" when contracted becomes "must've." To the ear, this sounds exactly like "must of." Writers who don't read don't know this and end up writing "must of" instead of "must've." A lot of students still think that "alot" is one word; it is not. And I despise the currently popular word "attitude" because it is so utterly meaningless. A student once wrote on a paper that in *Uncle Tom's Cabin*, Simon Legree "had an attitude problem." Surely, one can get more specific. A student complained once in class that my picking on her grammar showed that I had an attitude. I replied, "What kind of an attitude do you mean? Happy? Sad? Angry? Frustrated?" "Well," she said, putting her hand on her hip, "you certainly do have an attitude!"

CHAPTER 11
Punctuation

The Comma

This little cur causes more problems than it should. There are some basic rules that help govern the use of the comma; once learned, these rules will work 90% of the time.

1. The most common comma error has to do with the use of the comma to separate two parts of a sentence. Just to review the basics, a sentence must have both a subject and a verb; sometimes it has an object as well. If you have two such sentences connected by a conjunction like "and," then you must put in a comma before the connecting "and." Other such conjunctions include "but," "for," "yet," and "nor." If either of the sentences could not stand alone without the support of the other, then you do <u>not</u> put in the comma. For instance:

"Mary kicked her boyfriend and then shot his dog."

In this sentence, "and then shot his dog" cannot stand alone as a sentence because it has no subject. It depends upon the subject of the first sentence, Mary. Hence, no comma is put before "and."

In "Mary kicked her boyfriend, and then she shot his dog," the sentence "then she shot his dog" can stand alone. Hence, a comma is required before the "and." In more complicated sentences, you may have to stop and think to figure out if a subject is there or not. But that is the point. The writer needs to do that so the reader will not have to. Any time a reader is forced to reread a sentence to figure it out, the writer is doing a bad job.

2. The second most troublesome use of the comma comes when a phrase within a sentence has to be separated from the rest of the sentence. To many students, the distinction seems totally arbitrary. It is not. Consider this sentence:

"My grandmother who smokes pot is eighty."

Would you or wouldn't you put commas around "who smokes pot?" The answer is that you can do either; it depends entirely on what you mean to say. That is the important reason for going to all this trouble. Including the commas changes the meaning. If you don't know that, it's as if you were writing in a foreign language you do not understand. Imagine the possibilities for disaster!

Without commas, this sentence says that of your two grandmothers it is the pot-smoking one who is eighty. (The bourbon-drinking one, presumably, is ninety-two.) Without commas, the phrase, as we say, is restrictive. It is there to indicate specifically which grandmother you are talking about.

With commas, "My grandmother, who smokes pot, is eighty," implies that you have only one grandmother who (by the way) smokes pot and is eighty. The commas separate out extra material that is added to the sentence but is not necessarily crucial to the main point, which is your grandmother's age. You could say "My grandmother is eighty," and the basics of the sentence would remain. You would, however, have just killed off your ninety-two-year-old bourbon-drinking grandmother. Way to go!

Another example of this same principle occurs when you are citing an author's books. Robert Frost's poem "Stopping by Woods on a Snowy Evening" is a well-loved poem. Writing it this way, without commas around the name of the poem, specifies which of Frost's poems you are talking about. It is restrictive. If you put in commas and write "Robert Frost's poem, 'Stopping by Woods...'" you are saying that Robert Frost wrote only one poem which (by the way) is called "Stopping by Woods..." See?

The same principle applies elsewhere. "He stopped in Fairfax, Virginia, by mistake." Always put commas around the state or country so designated. This is because you are saying that Fairfax is (by the way) in Virginia. It is an extra bit of information. I find that saying (by the way) to myself helps me to determine whether any particular phrase ought to or ought not to have commas around it.

For those who relish the finer distinctions, this is also the reason for sometimes using "that" and othertimes using "which." You use "which" when the information in the phrase is incidental to the main idea. You use "that" when the information is important and restricts the meaning of the main thought. When you use "which," you should be able to think "(by the way)."?

3. Things in a series need to have commas: "He, she, and I." Some teachers allow the second comma to be omitted; not I. It is there to avoid confusion. Use it. Also, in a list of adjectives before a noun, if the word "and" can be inserted but is not, use commas: "the green, ugly, scum-covered lake."

4. Introductory and final phrases which [Whoops! should be "that"] might cause confusion or create ambiguity should have commas: "Heading

for the green, Dad forgot his golf clubs." Note that without the comma the reader would automatically read "Heading for the green Dad...."

5. Other uses of the comma include

— a direct address when the person's name or title is included: "Love me, daddy, all night long."
— before a quote: He said, "My heart is aflame or is it gas?"
— contrasted elements set aside: "I asked for a piece of pie, not pizza pie, when I called."

Note that in all of these, the underlying rule is to avoid ambiguity and confusion. Use the least amount of punctuation needed to keep your meaning clear. If you are not sure if you need a comma, try to imagine how another reader might misunderstand your intent if the commas were left out.

Semicolons

My best advice on semicolons is not to use them at all. I rarely see them used correctly on college papers, and they are rarely necessary. Faulkner could not have written without them. But you are not Faulkner, and Faulkner was not writing for an undergraduate English class.

If you must know, used correctly the semicolon substitutes for a period to join two closely related ideas. In other words, it should not be used to set off phrases at either end of a sentence that could not otherwise stand alone as independent sentences. So why not use a period? "I am going to the library; Jill is going to the market," is an example of the proper use of a semicolon. "Jill is going to the market; the one near the end of town" is an example of the incorrect use of a semicolon. One most often sees semicolons connecting two phrases that are joined in contrast to each other; however, this convention is overused.

Phrases in a series also take semicolons instead of commas if there are commas within the phrases. This helps to separate the things that are being serialized from the extraneous information. For instance, when I am grading papers, I like to sit in a chair, a green one; to use a red pen, preferably a felt-tip; and to torture small animals, either hamsters or mice.

Colons

I always think of these two dots as two hands outstretched palms up saying "and here they are." Colons are thus used to introduce things in a list or a quotation that is not otherwise introduced. "Many things are found in the sea: clams, mermaids, and hospital syringes." But if you have a phrase like "such as," you do not use the colon. The colon takes the place of the introductory phrase. In a quotation, the same distinction applies. "Emerson said, 'A foolish consistency is the hobgoblin of little minds.'" But "There is an Emersonian phrase that is much quoted: 'A foolish consistency is the hobgoblin of little minds.'" In the second example, the colon can be thought of as saying "and here it is."

Quotation Marks

The rule regulating the use of quotation marks is fairly straightforward: only put quotation marks around actual, literal quotations. Some students have begun to use quotation marks for emphasis; off with their heads! Use the double quotation marks only on either side of a statement that you can prove is an actual quotation, word for word. If the original is ungrammatical or misspelled, quote it exactly. If you want to protect yourself from the charge that you left in a typo which in fact is not yours, put [sic] in brackets after the quoted word. This is Latin for "So." It means, "Hey, prof, this author actually said it this way. It's not my fault. And I've got the proof if you need it." Note that parentheses within a quote are considered part of the quote. Only brackets indicate an intrusion into the quotation.

There was actually a case in the courts recently in which a writer put quotation marks around words not actually said in an unflattering book about a man who subsequently sued the author. A lot of writers who should know better defended the practice on the grounds that the distinction between fact and fiction is so subjective that it does not matter. This is an example of the literary world's desire to believe that language, its language, constitutes reality, that there is no truth outside of language and since all such "truth" is really a language construction, then any language construction is as good as any other. The courts decided otherwise.

The biggest problem I've run into with quotation marks on student papers is placement of any punctuation not part of the quote. Once upon a time, the rule regulating this was easy to follow. All punctuation went within the quotation marks whether it was part of the quotation or not. Did Nixon really say "I am not a crook?" Note that the question mark is not part of the quote, but still it resides inside the quotation marks. The only exceptions to this rule were the colon and the semicolon. Absolutely everything else went inside the quotation marks no matter what the circumstances.

You undoubtedly have noticed the nervous use of the past tense in this explanation. During the year I was in Slovakia imparting the glories of American culture to the victims of Marxism, someone changed the rules on me. I still have not figured out who or why. But the latest editions of the college handbooks have allowed question marks not part of the quotation to go outside of the quotation marks. Hence, my example above now should be written, Did Nixon really say "I am not a crook"? I have been told that this change follows the change in printing technology from mechanical presses to computerized printing. When hot type was used, that is when little letters made of lead were covered with ink to imprint the letters on paper, the ink often would not cover the lonely little punctuation marks outside of the quotations. So the word went forth that henceforth all punctuation must go inside the quotation marks to satisfy the needs of the machines of production. Marx would've loved it. But what once was required in printing can now be changed. Printers no longer use hot type but instead use computers, and computers can do anything. Hence, the old rule may be changed in favor of more rational considerations. This is another example of how our language is constantly changing. In American culture, nothing ever stays the same. Prepare to be flexible and stay tuned.

Note also that a quote within a quote gets single quote marks to distinguish it from the surrounding quotation. This is the only instance in which single quote marks are to be used. For some reason, more and more students are using single quote marks by themselves within their papers. I don't know why. But it's wrong.

Parentheses ( ), Brackets [ ], And Dashes –

All of these are overused.

Parentheses are used to insert material into the text that is out of context. Most of the time, such material should either be omitted entirely or brought into the text in its own sentence or paragraph if it is important enough. Students too often use this device to jam extra information into the text in the hope that quantity will outweigh quality in the grade book. It won't.

Brackets are used primarily to insert material into the middle of a quote that is not actually part of the quote. If Cotton Mather has some brief line of Greek and you want to include your translation within the quote, then put your translation directly after the Greek in brackets. Otherwise, don't use brackets.

Emily Dickinson used dashes instead of punctuation. But she was not writing either for publication or for a college assignment. Besides, she was crazy. Students who use dashes are either indulging in a lazy habit or trying to show off. The point of a college paper is to prove that you know how to do it right. Strictly speaking, dashes perform the same function as parentheses, so play it straight and use regular punctuation. There will be plenty of opportunities to be creative after you graduate.

CHAPTER 12
Citations, Endnotes, and Footnotes

Here we get into the tedious and technical yet necessary business of citing your facts and quotations. The rules have changed since I was in college, and some of my colleagues have not kept up. Therefore, not all of your professors in the humanities will expect the same system. Be sure to inquire before handing in your term research paper. The new system is known as the MLA (Modern Language Association) system, and it is that which I recommend here.

First, all direct quotations must be cited. Anytime you use another person's exact words, you must acknowledge the citation. Block quotes are the most common example. Anytime you quote more than four typed lines of prose, you must separate the quotation from the rest of your text. Leave a blank line before the block. Leave ten spaces on the left but no extra spaces on the right. The citation goes at the end. Better than the padding of a series of block quotes is the excision of telling phrases from within that quote that are then included within your text and not blocked. When possible, the citation here goes at the end of the sentence, but if there is any possibility of confusion, put the citation right after the quote, within the sentence rather than at its end.

The citation itself requires the name of the author and the number of the page on which the quotation was found. This information appears within parentheses and without punctuation. A line from Smith's *History of Virginia* might be followed by (Smith 13). The idea is to provide the least amount of information in the text that will allow the reader to find the citation in the back of your paper on the "Works Cited" page.

The "Works Cited" page is basically a bibliography. There, all of the works you used or cited or both are listed alphabetically by the authors' last names. Hence, the reader ought to be able to run down the first column on the page through the last names until the name "Smith" appears. If there is only one Smith, then the entire citation for that book should be there. The reader already knows that the quote is from page 13. If there are two books by the same Smith, then the writer needs to add information in the parenthesis that will most quickly make the distinction clear. The first word of the two titles if different should do it. Hence, the citation might have to read

(Smith <u>History</u> 13) as opposed to (Smith <u>Cooking</u> 33). If there are two different books by two different Smiths, then the citation will have to include the first name as well as the last to make the distinction. The citation then might read (Smith, John 13) as opposed to (Smith, Tim 22). Whatever gets the reader to the right citation the fastest is correct.

Note that the punctuation falls outside the parentheses. The point of the parentheses is to separate the information from the surrounding sentence; it is thus within that sentence. A citation at the end of a sentence has a period to the right (Williams 83). Question marks also should go to the right. I have however seen cases even in the handbooks where a question mark came before the parentheses, but even these were followed by a period after the parentheses to make it clear which sentence the parentheses were within.

On the "Works Cited" page, simply list the works in alphabetical order by the last name of the author. Give the full title, the publisher, the publication date of the exact copy of the text you cited from, and the city of publication. The reason for the citation is to allow a suspicious professor to check on your citation. You must therefore refer to the exact edition. The wording sometimes changes. Scholars are always finding new evidence of authorial intent that was mangled by some hamhanded or prudish printer. Even such classics as Emerson's "Nature" and Twain's *Huckleberry Finn* have recently undergone change.

There are too many variables in this format to list here. For all of the many possibilities, refer to a standard handbook, preferably *The MLA Style Manual*. Newspaper articles, encyclopedias, film and video tape, etc. all have different rules for citation. If you remember the reason for the citation, you will probably not get in trouble. Provide the reader with a way to get from the quotation in the text to the actual source as quickly and easily as possible. That is all.

Quotations, of course, are not the only things that need to be cited, but they are the most frequent. If you use an idea that someone else is responsible for, you should cite it. If you use a fact that might be questioned, even if you do not put anything in quotes, you should cite it. On the other hand, if you use facts or ideas that no one will question, don't bother citing them. This is a subjective decision that you must make. But if you say in your text that Dan Quayle was a member of the Communist Party in his youth, you had better provide a citation so we can check your sources.

Be sure to use credible sources relevant to your subject and do not depend on one book or one particular point of view. You may have picked up a book by some paranoid Larouchie or worse. Know who your sources are and what their biases are. I once had a student turn in a paper on arms control in which every footnote was a reference to some speech by Phyllis Schlafly. I flunked him. If writing about the Arab-Israeli struggle, do not use books by Arabs or Israelis exclusively. Do not write about South Africa without taking into account the position of the Afrikaaners. Include several views.

One problem of mine with the new MLA system is that it does not allow for an easy and consistent use of what I call "chatty endnotes." Sometimes we want to put extraneous information in a note and not in the text. For instance, we may want to thank our spouses and children for not interrupting us so we could write our precious monographs. Or we might want to cite thirteen other books on the topic which failed to get the point. Or we might want to include some special pleading. All of these are legitimate and fun. I have read several academic books in which such footnotes were the only good parts. In this case, you need to create a second page titled "Notes." And in your text, when you want to refer to one of these asides, you must use the old super-script 1, 2, 3, etc. This is clumsy and makes the new system more complex rather than simpler. It imposes a second overlay of notation upon your text. Perhaps you should simply leave chatty footnotes to chatty professors, and either leave the information out if it is unimportant or include it in your text.

This new MLA system is still under development. In American English, nothing is ever written in stone. Be sure to ask your professor what he or she prefers. For instance, unlike the MLA, I see no reason to include a lengthy bibliography that basically duplicates the "Works Cited" page. I tell students to include each of their reference works on the "Works Cited" page even if they do not have a citation to it. That way, this page can serve as a bibliography too.

CHAPTER 13
A Sample Quiz – Just For Fun!

Each of the following sentences, most of which came from papers I have graded, has some problem or problems. Locate the error and correct the sentence. Then, and only then, look at the next page for the real poop.

1. Southpaws, who are superstitious, will not pitch on Fridays.

2. College students who do not write well flunk English.

3. As a student, Aunt Normies' dinners are to be avoided.

4. What we need are some engineers broken down by their specialties.

5. As a boy games of war are fun.

6. We drove to Reno Nevada to gambol.

7. Phil is the only one of the swimmers who has won two gold medals.

8. She wasn't aloud to have friends over their house.

9. The blacks banned together to oppose segregation.

10. Hopefully, you will pass the test, otherwise I will feel badly.

11. Literally climbing the walls, I scream as another misplaced modifier appeared on the term paper and I decided to immediately give up teaching, and became a sadistic killer.

1. This sentence literally says that all southpaws are superstitious. Unless this is what the author intended, the sentence should not have the commas but should be restrictive.

2. This sentence is probably correct. To surround the who phrase with commas would be to say "College students, who (by the way) do not write well,..." But a few college students do write well, even today, so the sentence is better as it stands.

3. This is a classic MM. Aunt Normie's dinners are not "a student." Nor should there be an apostrophe after the s unless her name is Normies, which I doubt.

4. Are the engineers being broken down? That is what the sentence actually says. What we really need is a list of engineers, and the list needs to be broken down by the engineers' specialties.

5. This is another MM. The games are not "a boy."

6. "Nevada" needs to be separated out by commas, and "gambol" should probably be "gamble."

7. Should it be "who has" won two gold medals or "who have" won two gold medals? The answer depends on whether the who refers to the singular Phil or the plural swimmers. Since Phil is the only one who won two gold medals, the who seems to be refer to Phil. Thus, it is Phil who "has won" the trophies.

8. "Aloud" is misspelled; the word is "allowed." The phrase "over their house" suggests that her friends are birds. This is a colloquialism the language could do without.

9. "Banned" is misspelled; the word is "banded." Be careful!

10. "Hopefully" is always a problem; use it at your risk. The second comma is a classic comma splice holding two separate sentences together. Use a semi-colon or a period. And to "feel badly" means to be clumsy with your hands. It should say "feel bad."

11. Do not say "literally" unless you are a fly. The tenses here need to be consistent. If "scream" is left in then "appeared" has to be in the present tense also, as do "decide" and "become." Since these are two complete sentences joined by a conjunction, "and," there should be a comma after "paper." If you want to leave the comma out, eliminate the "I" also. "To immediately give up" is a split infinitive. The comma after "teaching" is inappropriate since the final phrase cannot stand alone as an independent sentence.

IN CONCLUSION

Try to remember and believe that the purpose of writing is to communicate ideas as clearly and as quickly as possible. Do not try to show off, or confuse, or pontificate. Do not be afraid to let your ideas stand boldly and clearly on the page. Writers who clothe their ideas in layers of elaborate silk and satin are hiding the reality underneath, not beautifying it. Away with their verbal fig leaves!

Remember that we are all sinners, naked before God; none of us really knows the answers. We are all groping in the dark. Academic tyrants and bullies will try to pretend that they know, that they are superior beings entrusted with some secret TRUTH. They will try to terrorize you into lies and confusion. Don't let them. Of course you might be and probably are wrong, but so are they. So speak your own ideas with clarity. Emerson at least had the right approach: "To believe that what is true for you in your private heart is true for all men; that is genius. Speak your latent conviction and it shall be the universal sense." Therefore, Sin Boldly! Stand fast in the liberty of the spirit and be not entangled again in the yoke of bondage.